The tips for success and the hands-on approach are *unsurpassed*. I am more sure of my success now than ever before.

—**Kathleen Johnson, BA, AICI, POC, president, RIM**

After *Guerrilla Marketing* became a best-seller, the series took on a life of its own ... irrevocably tied in with the unconventional, non-textbook, and practical wisdom of guerrilla business practices for small business.

—***Home Office Computing***

This has been an amazing experience ... I now have a *direction and stronger vision* to reach my destination.

—**K. Torrance, account manager, CJAY 92, VIBE 98.5**

I have seen the effect that these clear and distinct principles have had in my office—people are actually different and doing wonderful things. We have real measurable results.

—**Lorna Gardner, Toronto, Ontario**

With my new vision, the possibilities are endless.

—**Linda L., Remax Realty**

You exceeded my expectations, entertaining and informative.

—**Ken Foster, general manager, CTC Train Canada**

There were specific ideas that could easily be applied in real life.

—**Claire Beaudoin, manager, Pro Alta Consulting**

Other books, films, and audios by Douglas Vermeeren

Books

365 Daily Lessons from Amazing Success
Millionaire Wisdom
Guerrilla Millionaire
Guerrilla Masterminds
How Thoughts Become Things
The Opus
The Gratitude Experiment

Films

The Opus (www.TheOpusMovie.com)
The Gratitude Experiment (www.Gratitude-experiment.com)

Hire Douglas Vermeeren to speak at your event.

Douglas Vermeeren is The Sales Trainer. His techniques and strategies have been helping companies and individuals sell better, sell easier and sell more! He is the author of several books on growing business and sales and is a regular featured expert on FOX, FOX Business, ABC, NBC, CNN, CTV and CBC.! For more information call 1-844-486-7355

For a complete list or to order these programs, go to:
www.DouglasVermeeren.com or call 1-877-393-9496.

*Over 21,000,000 Guerrilla Books Sold
in Sixty-Two Languages Worldwide!*

Guerrilla Achiever

The Unconventional Way to Become Highly Successful

Douglas Vermeeren

Foreword by Jay Conrad Levinson

Warning:
*This book contains guerrilla tactics and tools
to help you get to your goals and create lasting
success in the most accelerated way possible!*

iUniverse®

GUERRILLA ACHIEVER
THE UNCONVENTIONAL WAY TO BECOME HIGHLY SUCCESSFUL

iUniverse books may be ordered through booksellers or by contacting:

iUniverse LLC
1663 Liberty Drive
Bloomington, IN 47403
www.iuniverse.com
1-800-Authors (1-800-288-4677)

Because of the dynamic nature of the Internet, any web addresses or links contained in this book may have changed since publication and may no longer be valid. The views expressed in this work are solely those of the author and do not necessarily reflect the views of the publisher, and the publisher hereby disclaims any responsibility for them.

Any people depicted in stock imagery provided by Thinkstock are models, and such images are being used for illustrative purposes only. Certain stock imagery © Thinkstock.

ISBN: 978-1-4917-2915-1 (sc)
ISBN: 978-1-4917-2916-8 (hc)
ISBN: 978-1-4917-2917-5 (e)

Library of Congress Control Number: 2014904973

Printed in the United States of America.

iUniverse rev. date: 06/17/2014

Acknowledgments

Special thanks to my wife, Holly Vermeeren, for her patience while I put together the manuscript and her suggestions, which no doubt made it better.

I want to thank all who helped with the creation of this book and opening the doors to make this project possible: Amy Levinson, Jill Lublin, Douglas Van Voorst, Megan Christmas, Rachel Dobson, Garret Roberts, and all the top achievers who gave me the opportunity to interview them. And thanks for the great friendships we have continued since then. You are all so amazing!

I especially want to thank Jay Conrad Levinson for allowing me to do this book and having the confidence in me to deliver the goods.

I have been a fan of the Guerrilla Marketing series since opening my very first business in the late 1990s. The Guerrilla Marketing series has been my favorite resource for finding practical solutions to deal with real-life situations in business and creating my successes. The Guerrilla Marketing books have definitely proven that they are the very best resources available.

I am proud and honored to now be a part of the Guerrilla Marketing family.

Thank you, Jay.
Douglas Vermeeren
Calgary, AB Canada

Contents

Foreword
by Jay Conrad Levinson,
The Father of Guerrilla Marketing

There are many fine books out there on achieving, each one specializing in one aspect of true achievement. This book specializes in the entire topic of achievement, and it's not as simple as you may have been led to believe. There is no single key to success.

But in these pages reside all the keys to achievement and success. None should be overlooked. You won't make it to the top of many ladders if several rungs are missing. None are missing here.

You'll see, fast enough, that achieving is not a goal you attain, but a habit you develop. In addition to the four Ps of achievement—potential, possibilities, probabilities, and performance—you'll gain insight into four more Ps: practice, patterns, preparation, and purpose. All will help you make achievement part of your life.

The first book I wrote was written on one Saturday afternoon, self-published, had thirty-six pages, and was sold for one dollar. By now, I've authored or coauthored fifty-eight books, most by major publishers, each taking at least six months or more to write, and at last count, resulting in sales of twenty-one million copies in sixty-two languages. Unconsciously, I've been following the laws of achievement over four decades. You won't have to wait that long. Armed with the glowing brilliance in this book, you'll probably earn more money than me. We sure hope that happens. That's our plan for you in this book.

One of the secrets of success of the Guerrilla Marketing books has been their ability to take a complex subject and make it primer simple. This book does the very same. By including the wisdom of many exceptionally high achievers and studying the achievement patterns of others, this book sets down a fail-safe pattern for your own achievement.

It's like connecting the dots in a drawing. Connect the dots in this book and you'll reveal to yourself a masterpiece for your own life. I can guarantee that you'll have a glorious time discovering the dots in this book. The true stories from the lives of the author and the excerpts from success interviews with fascinating and successful people are so captivating that you'll resent the author for ending the book.

It's that much fun and that easy to read.

But the book doesn't come to an end at all. Instead, it comes to rest—vibrant and alive—in your soul, just raring to go. For you, it's a beginning. As everyone knows, some people learn all there is to know, but the information stays in the wrong place—inside of them. Who does the world belong to? It belongs to those who take action.

Achievement isn't a process of learning as much as it is a process about doing.

So what are you waiting for?

Jay Conrad Levinson
DeBary, Florida

Douglas Vermeeren—The Modern-Day Napoleon Hill
by Stan Romero

In 1993 Douglas Vermeeren was a broke college student barely getting by with support from his parents. It was over that summer that he accepted a job selling pest control in California. At first his results were less than extraordinary, but soon he found a golden key that unlocked an abundant future that he hadn't even imagined. That key was a book called *Think and Grow Rich*, by Napoleon Hill.

To write the book, Napoleon interviewed more than four hundred of the world's top achievers in his day. His top achievers included people like Henry Ford, Thomas Edison, Andrew Carnegie, and others.

As Vermeeren read *Think and Grow Rich,* he began to put into practice many of the success strategies that were listed there. But that was not enough for him. As he read he was intrigued by the personal stories that Hill shared from his interactions with these top achievers. It was then that Vermeeren decided that it was one thing to read about top achievers, yet quite another to study directly under them. He set out on a mission to conduct extensive firsthand research of the top achievers of today.

There would be two major differences between how Napoleon Hill studied success and how Douglas Vermeeren would do it. First, a lot had changed since Napoleon Hill wrote *Think and Grow Rich* in 1937. In 1937 the top business leaders were inventors and innovators, businessmen who had built their enterprises from concept to creation, mavericks, so to speak, on the landscape of frontier business America. Vermeeren wanted to include new business models like multinational corporations, technology companies, publicly traded companies, and even companies in the direct marketing fields. Vermeeren also included another category that Napoleon

Hill neglected to study—celebrities and athletes. When Hill originally conducted his research, celebrities and athletes were not what they are today. Now an individual celebrity is considered a brand, with an organization behind him or her, commanding millions of dollars for a single appearance in a movie or television show.

Vermeeren's research took the better part of ten years. Within these pages you will find insights that he has gained through his research with some of these top achievers. Some excerpts from his studies are also contained within this volume.

Vermeeren's research is an important contribution to modern personal development on several levels. No one since the days of Napoleon Hill has actually gone out and done the research into the world's elite to determine how success is created. Vermeeren's findings are real-world strategies that have a proven track record for results. Too often authors, coaches, and speakers today are only sharing what they've learned in books or through someone else's experience. In many ways, that's like making a photocopy of a photocopy of the information they teach. With Vermeeren, you are drinking as close to the original source as you can get. It's not surprising to see that organizations like ABC, FOX News, and others are calling Douglas Vermeeren the modern-day Napoleon Hill.

Success, as you will find within these pages, does not come by accident. It requires hard work and the correct formula to work at. That is what you'll find in *Guerrilla Achiever.*

Enjoy,
Stanley T. Romero
Chicago, Ill

1—The Achievement Process

That some achieve great success,
is proof to all that others can achieve it as well.
—Abraham Lincoln

All human beings have amazing potential to accomplish incredible things. Think about it. Marvelous things are achieved in nearly every endeavor of human experience.

We have discovered medical cures and procedures that prolong life and cure disease. We have journeyed to and discovered distant lands. And now we have even begun to explore planets other than our own.

Our accomplishments are grand, and what we are attempting seems to be coming toward us faster and with more convenience, intensity, and comfort than ever before.

Human athletes have set records, only to be broken shortly thereafter by others who would run faster, climb higher, jump farther, and push themselves harder than was ever thought possible.

Financial prosperity among us has also grown. One scholar observed that in the year 1900 there were only five thousand millionaires in America. One hundred years later, in the year 2000, it was found that we now had more than 5 million millionaires. (And it is incredible to notice that most of them were self-made inside of a short time span of only ten years.) Experts are now predicting that the number of millionaires will continue to increase by another ten to twenty times this current number in the next twenty years.

Isn't it incredible to see such amazing results? The message to us is clear. Incredible opportunities to create success are available to everyone. Anything you seek after can be attained if you follow the right path to get there.

Is it that easy?

Perhaps you have been frustrated, like me, to find that it is not that easy. Many motivational teachers are very quick to boost your confidence and tell you, "*Yes*! You can do it! You can do anything!" But when you get home, you discover it's not as easy as it sounded in the seminar.

Let's be honest. Just hearing about how others are successful does not give you all the tools to be able to do it too.

It reminds me of a T-shirt I bought. It has a dirt-bike rider flying through the air performing an amazing stunt. The caption under the picture reads, "I saw it on TV. I am pretty sure I can do it." I have seen lots of stuff on TV, and quite frankly, much of it I know I could never do.

In this volume I want to give you a more valuable message. I want to share with you *how* you can achieve—really achieve—a lasting feeling of success in your life.

Each one of us has the seeds of great accomplishment, possibility, and potential within us. But that doesn't mean we can all do it instantly. In my research of more than four hundred of the world's top achievers, I found that there are specific things that top achievers do. And while it isn't that mysterious, it's just not being talked about.

The purpose of this book is to give you those tools on how you can be successful and maximize the results in your life.

That's what *Guerrilla Achiever* is all about. As it states in the subtitle, much of what I am going to share will be unconventional.

These methods are unconventional.

They are not a quick, easy, instant change.

The two most significant things I found in creating lasting success are:

1) It takes time and practice.
2) It takes a correct pattern.

If you get started right and you have correct expectations, you can do amazing things. Your expectation should be that it will take time and practice and you will have to learn the correct pattern of what to do.

All growth starts with time, practice, and a correct pattern.

Too many people overlook the elements of time and practice. They want everything right now, and they don't expect they have to gain any skills or qualifications to get there. If by chance they recognize that they need a pattern to follow, they often don't have a clue what it is.

The pattern or formula is crucially important. You've probably heard the often-expressed analogy that if you want to see a sunrise, you may run west as fast as you can, but you'll never see it. You are going in the wrong direction. The same is true for creating success; the pattern or formula to accomplish a specific achievement must be specifically correct.

Anything significant you will ever attain in your life will not come by accident. It will require deliberate and consistent effort. And the more effort you put into getting results, the more you will experience success. Getting to lasting success is not like turning an on/off switch on a light. Instead, it is more like a dimmer switch, where things will appear brighter and brighter gradually as you put in the effort and work to get there.

Lasting success will be established over time as you apply and practice these principles and get better at them.

Can you imagine if success were granted in any other way? Let's say, for example, my goal were to be a heart surgeon and you were my patient.

How would you feel if I told you I was an instant success and just started yesterday? No doubt you'd never let me operate on you. Some things just take time. When was there ever an expert who just started yesterday? It does not happen that way.

Life requires us to pay a price to qualify for success. Expert success can only come through quality and quantity practice. Time and practice are requirements! Having said that, there are some valid shortcuts and things that you can do to increase the probability of success in a shorter time frame, and we'll share some of those strategies shortly. But there is no substitute for hard work and practice.

Are the top achievers at odds with popular gurus?

As I began my studies of top achievers, I also began to buy every success book I could get my hands on. I visited used bookstores in cities across the United States, Canada, and Europe. I ordered rare out-of-print books and first editions. I attended seminars. I bought CD sets and DVDs. My home collection has more than three thousand books on the subjects of achievement and success, and I've read them all. It didn't take me long to identify some common lessons that were and are still being taught as the path to success.

I took my research from the books to see how these tools worked in real life compared to what top achievers were really doing in the real world. I actually expected that what the books taught would be confirmed in reality. After all, most of these books were written by experts.

Boy, was I ever surprised!

The real-life achievers didn't typically follow most of the instructions in any of the success books. They generally didn't subscribe to the traditional patterns of writing things down, making traditional action plans, setting dates, and creating checklists; not one of them kept a traditional vision board or woke up and started chanting motivational mantras and affirmations to start their days. What? You mean all of the expert authors got it wrong?

This question has occupied my thoughts, studies, and life for the last decade. It became my obsession. I began a quest to find the correct answers as to what did work.

Before I share what works, let me share where we got many of the systems and tools taught today. It's important to understand the history of these systems and why they don't work so later on you can understand and apply the tools that do work.

I knew these nonworking systems had been taught for quite some time. So I began to dig specifically into many of the older publications about achievement. It quickly became clear that the majority of what is being taught today was more or less pirated from these early sources. The more I traced the roots of achievement, the clearer the story became.

The current method being taught about goal achievement came from assembly-line manufacturing. In other words, if you want X results, you work backward, build a plan, assign a date and various tasks along the way, and presto, you will arrive at your results.

A system designed for automated manufacturing was applied to human beings.

A few significant problems immediately appear with applying this assembly-line manufacturing-style system to human beings. First, people are not assembly lines or machines. While this formula takes into account what one must do, it does not consider what one must become.

No success can be sustainable without the character attributes to support it. We must become successful internally before experiencing success externally. If the element of being is left out of the formula, no success is sustainable in the long term no matter what you are able to do in the short term.

We are human BEings, not human DOings.[1]

No success can be sustainable without the character attributes to support it.

The other important element of the assembly-line model that is difficult to apply to a single human (and we will address this later) is that an assembly line has a series of experts who get very good at specific jobs. If someone is trying to apply this traditional formula of goal setting, you are the assembly-line worker who must do every job. Failure and frustration follow in many cases because we cannot become an expert in all things.

I don't know about you, but there are certain tasks that I am just not interested in becoming good at. When I was in school, I was pretty good at creative writing, but I was far from an expert at calculus. Maybe you remember a similar experience?

Times have changed.

Great philosophers like Napoleon Hill did a fantastic job of analyzing the achievers of his day. He explored firsthand how pioneers and innovators like Henry Ford, Thomas Edison, John Rockefeller, Charles Schwab, and others of that early era created success. His lessons are still applicable today and are gems never to be discarded. Hill's work revealed a valuable series of repeatable patterns and lessons in powerful thinking to create lasting success in his day. But since that time, there has been much careful research that was not possible in Hill's day.

My studies have two major differences from the work done by Napoleon Hill.

The first major difference is that Hill primarily studied innovators and inventors. I expanded my research to include many business models that did not exist in Hill's day. I also included professional athletes, celebrities, and musicians in my research. In Napoleon Hill's day, people in these careers were not making the kinds of money that they do today. Today these industries are massive and influential in our society. I also included them because to become a top achiever in these fields is an incredible achievement.

Remarkably, many of these people began in circumstances similar to everyone else. Some of them even started from very difficult circumstances. Successful achievement is not an accident. It is a formula, recipe, or pattern. They all followed a similar course, and so can you.

Successful achievement is not a single event, but a series of developed or refined habits, utilizing opportunities to work together toward a single destination. Creating great accomplishments is a matter of putting the smaller things together in the right way. In this book I will show you how to do that. You'll also notice as you read this book that many of these success principles do not stand alone. They often overlap each other and must be used as a set of skills rather than individual items to produce results.

The way these principles work together could be compared to the spokes on a bicycle wheel. You can't really determine which should be the first and most important spoke. Each is important, and each must work together to make the wheel balanced and effective. If you only choose to apply one or two, you won't be riding your bicycle very long.

Success is gained by practicing and growing our capacity to implement correct principles.

With the speed of business and just about everything else today, I have designed this book to be easy to read and apply. Do your best to complete each exercise and grow each skill and make it active in your life. Ultimately it will be your ability to apply these lessons in real life that will make the biggest difference for you personally.

It is not enough to simply read it and say, "This was a nice book." Change happens when you get involved. To follow the analogy we started above, let's continue talking about bicycle spokes. When the spokes of attributes, habits, and characteristics are in place, the bicycle must then be placed on the road. A bicycle with complete spokes looks nice, but you won't get anywhere by just looking nice. You need to get on the road and start pedaling in the direction you chose to steer. That part will be up to you. You will get to decide where you will take the bicycle. You will choose the goals and destination you will travel to.

The road will have some familiar checkpoints.

There will be familiar checkpoints on the road to success and achievement, even though your destination may be different from anyone else's. These points are the journey that everyone follows on the route to accomplishment. Here is what the course to lasting success looks like:

The course to lasting success involves the four Ps of achievement.

Getting to success is not like a checklist of things to be accomplished and marked off. It is a process. Remember, as we said earlier, it is like a dimmer switch that will grow brighter gradually as you become more proficient on the course. I call this course the four Ps, and it's actually quite simple.
Here they are:

1) Potential. Any endeavor of significance must begin with us recognizing our potential and then tapping into that potential to begin. This includes beginning with an honest view of our starting point and is strengthened by a solid belief that we can arrive at the final destination. It includes the understanding that we are worthy of that final destination. Oftentimes people can feel inadequate at this stage, and that stops the entire process. Throughout this volume we will share some things that you can do to fortify your belief in your potential, such as preparation, acting with confidence, belief, faith, vision, and more.

Once you understand and believe in your potential, you will begin to see

2) Possibilities. Possibilities are best described as recognizing the opportunities that are around you. Oftentimes if your mind is not prepared to see opportunities, you will not recognize those possibilities. What we cannot see, we cannot do. Therefore without

recognizing possibility, nothing can change. You've maybe heard the saying that, "You can't get on a train if you don't know where the station is." Possibility is truly about recognizing opportunities to board the trains you would like to take. When we prepare ourselves and put ourselves in the best situations, opportunities become more obvious. Oftentimes we begin to see possibilities by just looking at things in a different way.

Once you have a target in mind of what is possible, you can create

3) Probabilities. Aristotle once said that, "What is most probable is what usually happens." Makes sense to me. The bulk of the effort of goal achievement really comes together in this stage. Successful achievement is a matter of effective problem solving. You are at point A and you want to get to point B. If you can solve the problem of transportation between the two points, you are successful. The same is true of any achievement. You must solve the problems or increase the probability of getting from where you are to where you want to go. Goal achievement is really about creating more and more probability that the goal will occur, and if you do that enough, you will eventually arrive. To be successful, you must ask the question "What can I do to make it more likely I will get to my goal?" It's almost like throwing darts at a dartboard. The closer you get to the bull's–eye, the more likely you are to get a bull's-eye. So what can you do to take continuous steps forward toward that bull's-eye? And the good news about probability is that you can increase it as fast as you like.

Yet increasing probability is not enough. Once you have the information and start to gain the experience that will lead you to your goal, what will you do with that information and experience?

Ultimately nothing changes unless you have

4) Performance. Performance is different from action. I chose the word intentionally. When the maestro in a concert hall gives a performance, he wastes no effort. He utilizes every instrument in

the most productive way to create the symphony. In describing this stage of performance, I also like to use the word *harmony*. Harmony is found when you find balance or get into your flow. Lasting success is about creating a harmony, balance, or equilibrium. If you have increased your probability correctly, you will already be a master at this to some degree. You will have experience to know what is harmony and what isn't. You will know what is giving you the most productive results.

Performance isn't just taking action. There are a lot of people out there taking action. They look very busy. But many of them just aren't getting anywhere. The action they are taking isn't producing the results that they are seeking, and in some ways they are just spinning their wheels. True success is not given to anyone just because he or she is busy; it is given to those who are most effective. In order for action to yield results, it must be effective action. Success is a prize that must be earned.

Throughout this book I will share some suggestions on how you can maximize your results, achieve more, and earn success. I congratulate you for deciding to make this journey. Let's begin.

(In addition to this volume, I also invite you to go to my website www.TheSalesTrainer.com of additional help on maximizing your results.)

2—Starting with You

It's not the mountain we conquer, but ourselves.
—Edmund Hillary

The price of greatness is responsibility.
—Winston Churchill

Have you ever looked through the window at a fitness club and spent some time watching all of the people training? Most likely you saw what I have seen.

People on the treadmill who seem to be able to run for miles and never run out of breath. Others pumping huge amounts of iron and with the bulging muscles to demonstrate they would have no trouble to even add a little more weight. I have seen other people in the swimming pool who glide through the water like otters, streamlined and in perfect form.

As you were looking through the window, have you ever wished that you could do those things?

Perhaps you have felt those feelings. My suspicion is that in most cases, those thoughts have not been enough to compel you to walk inside that fitness club and get started with a training program. Why not?

Simple. It is much easier to wish and dream than it is to open the door and get to work on making something happen.

The first step to accomplishing any task is to realize that just wishing and dreaming won't really change much. You need to act on those wishes and dreams. You must open the door to the fitness club, walk inside, and get to work. No one else can do that for you. How bizarre it would be to expect our muscles to grow by watching someone else do push-ups.

Our lives can only change as we accept responsibility to get personally involved in our personal development.

Are you really involved in your own life?

It has been said that accepting responsibility for our own situation is the difference between being a child or an adult. A child is satisfied to let others take care of his or her needs and give instruction for his or her daily activities. An adult, on the other hand, starts making decisions for himself or herself and gets to work to make those decisions a reality in his or her life. This can be seen in lives of successful people too. The more you choose to be responsible, the more you are in charge of your life. With that decision to be responsible come freedom and power to live your life in ways that you decide. Decide today which you will be—a child or an adult?

> If you are not engaged in becoming the person you want to be, you are automatically engaged in becoming the person you don't want to be.
> —Dale Carnegie

You must do something today.

It can be rare to find individuals who understand that they are in charge of their lives. That is really the beginning of being able to take charge of your life and create success. But just knowing the buck stops with you doesn't guarantee success or even a change. Some people know it's up to them, but they don't do anything about it. That's where the progress stops. These people often become paralyzed at the idea that there is too much to do, too far to go, and not enough time.

They feel they don't know enough or are not yet capable of doing anything that will make a difference for them. As a result, they do nothing. Perhaps they are waiting for a day that will make everything easier to do.

Well, here's the news flash: that day of instant ease will never come.

Much of your relationship with yourself is a learning experience.

When I think about my life, I realize that I have never discovered all of the answers at once. Things have unfolded gradually, and generally at the speed at which I am willing to act. I have to trust that I'll get answers as I go. Yet even without a clear picture of everything, I still see things that can be done immediately to make improvements today.

As you take greater responsibility for your situation, you will begin to recognize the patterns that you are currently engaged in. Some of these patterns are working, and some of them are not. You will recognize the situations you are creating. And this is primarily what is giving you the results you are currently experiencing. Recognition is a beginning to change. Starting from a place of truth is the beginning of progress. We can only change what we see and acknowledge.

Have purpose and be on purpose.

One of the differences between the most successful people in the world and those who are not as successful is their recognition of purpose. Unsuccessful people haven't really got one, while successful achievers have purpose in nearly everything they do. They are not aimlessly wondering and wandering. They have taken the time to determine what they want.

Armed with that knowledge, you will know what direction you need to go to get it. (Remember, in chapter one, we talked about increasing probability.)

Be responsible. Be on purpose. Be courageous and begin.

Be vs. Do

Actions speak louder than words,
but being speaks louder than actions.

Up until now, the results that you have been getting in your life have been a reflection of the patterns you have created in your life. In other words, your habits, choices, decisions, and actions have built for you your world.

These habits, choices, and decisions can all be traced back to your inner values and desires. In other words, your thoughts and actions are in the order of priority of what you value most. If you want different outward results, you have to begin by looking at your inward priorities.

Often people trade what they want most for what they want now. That is a reflection of their values. Immediate gratification is more important to many people than lasting results. Why is it that way?

Values

It really has to do with our values. Values shape the way we feel, believe, and see the world. Our values come to us in one of two ways: they are either absorbed or they are selected.

Absorbed values

Absorbed values are the values that enter our thinking and beliefs by the things surrounding us. Many of the values we learned as children are a result of our environment. We gain specific values from those who raised us—specifically from the way we were treated and the things we were told we could and couldn't do.

Many psychologists feel that the majority of absorbed values come from childhood experiences. Yet there is evidence that a portion of our values can change over time and that we are still absorbing values every day. The reason why these are called absorbed values is because we often do not realize that we are acquiring them. They are absorbed and become part of us without us ever becoming aware.

Selected values

Selected values are the values we actually choose. These enter our thinking because we have decided that we want them there. These specific values are harder to establish at times. They can require great effort to internalize and often require practice.

A misconception about selected values

It has been misunderstood by many that it can be an easy thing to change your values. It is not uncommon to hear gurus preach the idea that when you really want something (a selected value), you can easily create that as a new value. All you have to do is want that new value badly enough and it's yours. This is untrue.

The only way to establish a new selected value is by conducting a value trade. Let me explain this principle with the following example:

By the time you reach your early teens, you are like a full glass of water. The water inside represents your values. As I said, it is full, and there isn't room for any more water. It is full to the brim. The only way to get new water in is to get rid of some of the old water first. Only by being willing to exchange the old can we make room for the new.

Here is the value trade in action.

As you entered your teenage years, you began to trade childlike desires and values for ones that were now teenage-like. As you grew older, you began to trade your teenage-like values for ones that were more mature. Each time you gained new priority values, you had to let go of something you had valued as a priority before. Naturally this is a macro size example, but value trades happen on a smaller scale in our lives too.

The reason many people fail to create new and more successful situations for themselves is simply because the new life value does not have the power of an existing value that needs to be replaced. You cannot have a new value become your new priority direction unless it has more power.

Your values will dictate how you think, how you think will dictate how you feel, and what you feel most will dictate what you decide you are looking for and what you may want to change. What you decide is important you will focus on, what you focus on will affect what you do, and what you do will dictate what you ultimately get and become.

There is a formula for results that precedes every outside action:

Values and Beliefs > Thoughts > Feelings > Decisions > Focus > Action > Result

Values and Beliefs

Your values and beliefs are the channels through which your thinking must pass. Everything you think is influenced and sorted by what you value most and believe. It has also been said that every value is simply a thought that is held or believed long enough to become a value. These values and beliefs then become a filter that determines how we see future thoughts.

Thinking

Thinking is often defined as the mental processes by which our mind sorts our responses to external stimuli, or how we organize our internal reflections.

Generally our thinking seeks to validate our existing values. As we think about things that come into our path, they are sorted according to our values. Those values then gain more power because they appear to become more valid.

While there are many seminars and programs that suggest that your thinking can be changed at the snap of a finger, science has suggested that effective change is the result of consistent and continued effort and awareness.

Lasting change requires the establishment of new neural pathways in the brain. To build new neural pathways takes time and is often based on many factors, including the complexity of the new concepts or skills to be learned. How rapidly they can be adopted is also affected by how similar they are to existing neural pathways and habits. The closer they are to what you are already thinking increases the speed by which these new habits and thinking can be integrated.

Sometimes people may point to a change and think it was instant, but generally the elements to create that change have been brewing for a lengthier period of time.

Creating change can be comparable to melting an ice cube in your hand. It requires time for ice to melt, and while you are holding the ice cube, it is uncomfortable. As the ice melts, it leaves a void. The void that is left behind must be filled with something. That is why it is difficult for people to simply stop doing addictive behaviors like smoking, gambling, or overeating. That void must be replaced by something else of equal or greater value to the individual trying to make the change. If there is no increase in value, people tend to gravitate directly back to what it was they originally had or did.

Thinking has such a profound effect on the patterns in your life that it is important to consider some factors that contribute to your quality of thinking. In further chapters we will explore several strategies that will help to build more effective thinking and teach your mind the patterns of thought that successful people are using.

Feelings

When we experience a situation, the first involuntary reaction is what we feel. Our feelings are the result of what we value and what we think. An experience we have measures itself automatically by our values and the feelings that are produced. Our feelings immediately influence the judgments we make. When we feel positively or negatively about an experience, we begin to form beliefs and opinions about situations that were generated from that feeling.

Feelings based on previous experiences cluster together to form a pattern of thinking and reactions. The thinking and reactions they provoke create our results.

Decisions

Decisions occur all around us regularly. Many decisions affect us and influence what will occur in our lives. Often we are affected by the decisions of others. But the most powerful decisions must come from ourselves. If you want to master your destiny, you must decide what you want.

To be an effective decision for your success, you must make the choice.

It is true that in employment situations, others often dictate how you will spend much of your time. But the level of productivity, commitment, and diligence is significantly higher when the decision originates within you.

The influence of decision is so important that there is an entire section dedicated to decision farther on in this book, but for now it is important to understand that for decisions to be effective in the context of success and achievement, they must come from within and not from an outside source.

Focus

Focus is one of the most important principles of successful achievement and one of the major differences between people who get to their goals and those who fail.

My observations have been that those who fail to get to their goals either have focus but it's on the wrong thing or had focus at the beginning and could not keep it. Successful achievement cannot be attained without focus.

Unsuccessful people do not understand how to harness their focus. They have given themselves too many things to do. Too many trivial activities occupy their time, and they are spread too thin. As a result, the things that would give them the best results are often left undone.

Splitting focus is similar to trying to water a room full of plants with one glass of water. We only have so much energy and so many resources, mental and physical, that if we are trying to do everything, we are stretched too far. Focus is a matter of setting priorities and getting to work on the tasks that will give the best return.

Action

The last step in this pattern is to shift from the internal principles we've discussed so far to the external actions of doing. If we do nothing, we will get zero results. It's that simple.

I mention this here specifically because what we do must be closely attached to what we are. If our actions are not in harmony with our internal beliefs and values, we will fall out of harmony and we won't be happy.

Many people are frustrated with life simply because their actions don't measure up with their internal values. You can never be happy believing something and doing the contrary, even if it is for just a temporary gain. You cannot go against who you are and create a lasting success.

Often people get so caught up in what they are doing that they discover they have sacrificed what they are trying to become. In the end, what we are is ultimately more important than what we have.

If you ever were to lose the material things in your possession, you could build all of it again because of what you are. You would have the knowledge, attributes, and character traits that would enable you, most likely in a relatively short time, to build everything you initially had all over again.

And ultimately, what you have has a limited value anyway. You will lose it all at death. The only legacy you will truly leave for loved ones is the memory of what you were.

A leader

A study done on management and leadership in the early 1990s also confirmed the importance of being rather than doing or having. Part of the study involved a survey of more than ten thousand corporate employees to discover what they felt made the ideal leader.

While the survey allowed participants to consider education, financial status, past success experiences, and leaderships styles, these were not selected as the highest-rated traits in a leader. The most highly rated aspects of leaders were character- and attribute-based.

People were far more concerned about the kind of person or the attributes of the leader rather than what he had or had done previously. They wanted leaders with character.

As I have had an opportunity to interview people for positions with my company or consider possible business relationships, I always try to investigate whom I am hiring rather than just what he or she has in terms of education, background, and assets.

Howard Putnam, former CEO of Southwest Airlines, made a similar observation when we said, "At Southwest we hired attitudes; the rest can be taught."

BEing

We must *be* before we can *do* or *have*. Successful achievers begin inside.

There is a second benefit from beginning with an internal view of success. When we start from a place of being and becoming, we begin to have a clearer view of what success really is for us.

Exercise—The List

Not too long ago at a corporate training I was invited to conduct, I tried an interesting experiment. I had my ideas of what the outcome might be, but I wasn't really sure. I told the group that they would be part of an untried experiment.

I handed out pieces of paper to everyone and asked them to write down what they felt were their own greatest attributes. In other words, they were invited to list the strong points of their character and the attributes they felt others recognized in them. The pens got started and everyone soon had a list of a dozen or so things. I asked them to fold their list up without showing anyone and put it into their pockets.

I then had a second paper distributed, and a partner taped it to each participant's back. Everyone then walked around the room and wrote what attributes and characteristics they actually recognized in each other on the papers.

After the group had finished this exercise, we compared both sheets. It was interesting to see that there were some attributes that were the same, some that were dramatically different, and some that were new altogether. As a result, many of the participants were able to recognize strengths that they did not know they had and also recognize the areas where they thought they were strong but needed improvement.

We explored why some of these attributes were recognized and some were not, as well as what could be done differently to develop the attributes that individuals sought after. It was very enlightening.

No doubt there are areas where you perceive yourself very differently than others do. Wouldn't it be useful for you to know your true strengths versus the areas where you just think you are strong? Would it be interesting to see the strengths that you have that you don't yet see?

A solid foundation creates power that can be counted on.

When we start from a place of being, we are able to tap into the power of our own uniqueness and brilliance. We must discover what it is that makes us different and makes us brilliant.

Lots of teachers are encouraging people to get out of their comfort zones and discover things we are not good at. Quite frankly, I believe the opposite should occur. We don't need to spend all kinds of time developing things way out of our comfort zones.

You need to find your *brilliance zone*. Find what you are good at and become an expert there. You will do more, do better, and ultimately get more incredible results.

What about the stuff you don't do so well? Answer: find someone else who is brilliant in those areas outside your comfort zone and let them help you. (More on this later.) This concept of a *brilliance zone* is essential if you want to shift from average to extraordinary. You must learn how to delegate and focus on your strengths.

Think of it like this. Professional athletes focus on becoming the best when they play. That is their brilliance. To become the best, they must get extremely focused. They can't spend time trying to develop distractions that don't contribute to their playing skills. You need to play the same way. Focus on your brilliance, and your results will multiply!

Real success is often only known to yourself and a select few who understand who you really are. Successful is generally not something that is broadcast on TV and shouted from the housetops. You get to decide what it looks like, and you get to decide when you have arrived.

Exercise—Be vs. Do

Take a few moments and describe the person you want to be in your goal journal.

What kind of relationships do you want to have?

What attributes do you want to develop?

How do you wish to be perceived?

I have heard many authors invite their readers to write their eulogy for a funeral. I think this is a great idea. But I believe you should also write how you want to live today.

Consider how some of your daily activities should be lived in order to create better results. Be bold and write the ideal—not just what you think is realistically possible. What we consider realistically possible rarely gets people really excited. Make your ideal big and incredible.

With a view of who you wish to become, make some notes on things you can start to do *right now* that will enhance your ability to become that person.

Keep in mind that these changes will not happen instantly. Being aware of them will create greater power in your life for you to move in that direction.

Keep this outline nearby and review it often. Make a mental note of situations you encounter and where you could improve to bring your current actions into harmony with this future self.

Be vs. do—Questions to consider

- How would I describe my character and attributes?
- How would others describe me?
- What has happened in my life that demonstrates I have consistency?
- What can I do to create more consistency in my successes?
- What do I really want to be my end result?
- What thinking is required to change my current direction to resemble more closely my end result?
- What is preventing me from being what I want to be?
- What changes do I need to make immediately?

Preparation

The more we prepare, the luckier we seem to get.

Everywhere you look around in the world today, you can see the promise of overnight and easy success. Yet the truth is quite different: lasting success is never an immediate, instant, or just-add-water formula. Time, practice, and a correct pattern are always required. Essentially these ingredients can be called preparation.

In many ways preparation is like a key. A key can only open the locks it is designed to open. When an opportunity appears before us, if we are not prepared we will not be able to open that specific door until we have acquired the necessary preparation to possess that key.

The correct pattern involves taking advantage of opportunities.

I once saw *success* defined as the ability to take advantage of ideal opportunities as they appear. I think this is a good definition. Often opportunities slip past us, not because we won't participate, but because we can't.

Have you heard of people who have had golden opportunities to invest or participate in an incredible venture, but didn't because they could not afford to or because they heard about it too late? When you are prepared, you will begin to recognize more opportunities and be ready to participate when they appear.

It has been said that there are many empty chairs available at the top, but few are willing to make the climb to get there. Preparation is the key.

Some people leave things in their lives to chance and expect that everything will simply happen the way it is intended to. These people believe that things are genuinely out of their control. Nothing could be further from the truth.

The more we prepare, the luckier we seem to get. Preparation is an essential characteristic of success. How foolish it would be to expect success without preparing for it.

My friend Jim Tunney, who was one of the top referees in the NFL for thirty-one years, has seen many top athletes come onto the field. I found it interesting when he told me that professional athletes spent most of their time in preparation. For every hour on the field, there were countless hours in preparation.

I once saw an estimate that the average player spent approximately seventeen and a half hours in practice for every minute that he played during the season.

In all areas of life, the need for preparation remains the same. Without preparation we are not qualified to play with the best. And if we are lucky enough to get on the field without the required preparation, we will most likely not be invited back when we underperform.

"Success," Jim stated, "is a matter of taking care of the little things because you should already have the big stuff figured out. You just can't expect to walk into a job unprepared and have it go well for you."

We must be constantly on the lookout for things that will improve us and create a more-prepared self. The only difference between how realistic and unrealistic a goal is can be found in how well we are prepared.

Previous preparation

There are many talents and gifts that we have been preparing throughout our lives that we can utilize to create success. Many of the skills may go unnoticed by us until we need to use them. We must never overlook what tools we have already built in our lives thus far.

It is an important exercise to invest a little time to consider what positive attributes you already have and how they can lead you to greater success in the efforts you are currently making. Often these existing gifts can be applied to create great success if we take some time to consider how they might apply.

So what should I prepare?

It is one thing to say "get prepared." It is another to know what to prepare. I remember one time when I was a young Boy Scout. We had an important summer camp, and one of our leaders asked us, "Are you all prepared?" Everyone said yes, so I did too.

But inside I wasn't really sure if I was. I told my dad about the camp and then let him do the rest. My dad helped me pack most of my kit, but I didn't really pay attention as he put stuff in my pack and explained why I needed it. My mind was elsewhere during the packing process; when I got to the camp, I was surprised at what I found I had brought.

In fact, I found I had stuff I hadn't even considered I would need. If preparation had been up to me, I would not have been prepared.

Getting prepared is easier if you utilize the experience of others.

This taught me a valuable lesson in preparation. We need to consult and seek help from those with more experience and understanding in what we are trying to accomplish.

You may wish to consider places where you can get help with preparation, such as associations, work experience, volunteer opportunities, and more. These are all areas that will contribute to your preparation.

Volunteer opportunities? Why would I want to volunteer?

I have several friends who work in the television and broadcasting industry. One of the common aspects of their preparation was volunteer work. Most of them have been volunteers at local TV stations.

While they may not have gotten paid, they gained enormous amounts of real-life experience and formed relationships with those who could help them further their careers.

Chad Rutledge works in TV production, and this is what he said about the subject of volunteering. "I tried to get hired at first. Nobody would give me the chance. But when I volunteered, they were interested. And that's where things began to come together. Not only could I show them what I could do; I learned what I could not do, and why they couldn't hire me. My experience as a volunteer made me into someone hirable. And I eventually got the job I wanted."

While a volunteer, Chad also met the man who did the hiring for the station. They became close friends. And naturally when the job Chad wanted became available, he was immediately given the opportunity. His time as a volunteer was an investment toward acquiring the position.

Exploration

Volunteering is also an effort in exploration. I get a chance to work with a lot of groups, including teens, in the process of trying to discover what they want to do with their lives.

Some of them don't have a clue. I can relate to that. At their age I wasn't really sure what I wanted to do either. Many adults that I encounter are still in this situation. Either they haven't found what they want to do with their lives yet, or they have become stuck in doing something they don't like.

With all people I encounter trying to find where they fit, I encourage them to spend a week or two as a volunteer in a particular field of interest before committing to it.

If you want to be a veterinarian, volunteer at the animal clinic. If you want to be a lawyer, volunteer at a law firm. If you want to be a pilot, go and volunteer at an airplane hangar. If you want to open a business, go and spend some time in a similar business.

Here are some things you will learn from a volunteer experience:

- You will make contacts and form relationships.
- You will gain insights and education a textbook cannot teach.
- You will understand the correct course to get to your goal.
- You will get help with potential and current obstacles.
- You will find out if this is really something you want to do.

Preparation—Questions to consider

- Who can I consult regarding my preparation?
- What do I need to prepare?
- What am I doing to prepare today?
- What talents have I already nurtured that I can take advantage of?
- Who has experience that can help me?
- What groups or associations can I join?
- Where can I volunteer to learn more?

Excerpts from the Success Interviews: Jim Tunney, Ed D

Jim Tunney is an educator with twenty-eight years of experience as a teacher, coach, and principal at three high schools. He was also the superintendent of schools and member of the board of trustees at the high school and college level. But when people hear the name Jim Tunney, what comes to mind is an NFL Hall of Fame referee.

Considered the Dean of NFL Referees, Jim has spent thirty-one years as an NFL referee, participating in over five hundred NFL games, some of which are considered incredibly historic moments in sports, including: the Fog Bowl, Philadelphia at Chicago (12/31/88); the Final Fumble, Cleveland at Denver (1/17/88); the Snowball Game, San Francisco at Denver (11/11/85); the 100th Game, Green Bay at Chicago (11/19/83); the Catch, Dallas at San Francisco (1/10/82); the Kick, Detroit at New Orleans (11/08/70); the Ice Bowl, Dallas at Green Bay (12/31/67); the Field Goal, Baltimore at Green Bay (12/26/65); Super Bowl VI (1972); Super Bowl XI (1977); Super Bowl XII (1978); Super Bowl XVIII (1983).

For more information, check out www.JimTunney.com.

Doug: Hey, Jim, thanks for taking some time to chat this morning.

Jim: My pleasure, Doug.

Doug: For our readers, could you share in your own words a little bit about your journey, including where you began and some of the exciting highlights along the way.

Jim: I'd be glad to. My dad was a teacher and a coach for a while before he left education. I think since I was twelve, I wanted to be a teacher and coach; it was just something I wanted to do. I wanted to coach people, so I spent my youth in high school and college watching teachers, watching coaches. Seeing the good things they did, and the things I didn't think they did so well. And thinking gee, I don't want to do that when I get to be there, and learning from them. So as soon as I graduated from college, I was looking to get a teaching job and coaching job and became a head coach of a high school basketball team my first year out of college. That was a goal of mine.

I never wanted to write goals down. I organize them mentally. And think about it a lot, think about it constantly. It's really sort of a mental note that I'm making more than a written note. I know a lot of people talk about writing things down. I think that's a great idea for a lot of people, but for me it was just a matter of keeping it in mind all the time, and I had to focus on that. I decided I wanted to be a high school principal and worked my way through that process in the Los Angeles city schools for a time. I was in inner-city schools in my twenty-five years in Los Angeles. I was at the East LA school for thirteen years and West LA and Hollywood, always trying to think about how I could help people become better at what they do. My goal as a basketball, football, baseball coach or principal has always been to help kids get a better relationship with teachers, and vice versa, and help teachers become more effective in what they do.

Doug: So how did that journey, beginning as a high school principal in East LA, lead to becoming an official in the NFL?

Jim: When I was a teacher and a coach in college, I decided I would like to officiate, and I did some of that in college. My dad was also an official, so I had a leg up on that. I watched him. I went to games with him when I was a kid, like five, six, seven, eight, and nine. I thought that was a great opportunity to be involved in athletics and create an income, because I was making $12.50 for running a high school basketball game and I could work also for football and baseball as well. It started as a matter of a second income, and I loved doing it. Monday through Friday I was teaching, and Friday night or Saturday I was refereeing football or basketball games, and I worked my way in the Pacific West Conference, which is now called the

Pac-10. They saw me working there, and the NFL was expanding there with a number of teams in 1960 and so they asked me to join. I never even applied. They just asked me to join the NFL and I did, and I spent thirty-one years with them. It was a great opportunity for me.

I was at the right place at the right time, if I look back on it, and what helped is that I was ready. I was prepared. I had done high school, I had done the small colleges, I had done the major colleges. I just worked my way up, as I did in teaching. I worked my way up so that I could work with the best. When you got in the NFL, there was nothing better than that; that is the best of what there is.

Doug: Do you know exactly how many games it was that you were involved in?

Jim: Somebody figured out the other day that it was over five hundred NFL games that I refereed, and prior to that, I probably did seven hundred high school and college games.

Doug: There are a lot of prominent and historic games that you have been involved in. Of course, the Super Bowls too.

Jim: Super Bowl is a matter of working every day, every week, as you work and being evaluated, so that at the end of the season, you have high marks. That was always my goal: to have high marks and be the best at what I could be at the time. When you do that, then you get the Super Bowl, and the games that came along, like the Ice Bowl, the Kick, or the Catch. I was just being there at the right place at the right time.

Doug: I'm sure you didn't know they were going to be historic when you arrived there that day.

Jim: When they started the game, it was just a football game; at the end of the game, they became historic.

Doug: So what has been your most exciting moment?

Jim: When you work Super Bowl games, they are the greatest sports spectacles in the world. The great athletes, and being on the field with the best people. You name any player in the seventies, eighties, and nineties—I was on the field with them. Well, that's really fortunate. And not only the great players, but the great coaches. But if I had to settle for one, I would probably say Super Bowl XI, which was January 1977 in the Rose Bowl stadium in Pasadena. Mostly because I grew up just four miles from the Rose Bowl. As a kid I went to the Rose Bowl when my dad was there. I sat on the bench next to a guy named Jackie Robinson, who was playing for Pasadena Junior College at the time. I sat on the bench and watched him. I refereed the high school championship and college games there. The colleges have the Junior Rose Bowl game, which was between community colleges; I worked many games there. And when I had Super Bowl XI there, it was the first time they had taken the Super Bowl to the Rose Bowl. I got the assignment. Since it was the place where I grew up, I knew the stadium. I knew everything about it. It was an exciting time for me. After all those years, to come home, this was the place I started as a kid thirty or thirty-five years earlier.

Doug: Coming home. That's exciting. What was the hardest call that you ever had to make?

Jim: The other question that comes up is, Did you ever make a bad call? The answer to the question is, Did I ever make a bad call? No. I never made a call—I never made a call that I thought was bad. You never think, *Oh, here's a bad call, but I think I'll make it anyway.* You make it because you know it is right. You feel you're 110 percent sure it's right, but at the end of the game, it may not come out that way. It could be reversed on you. It may change. It may be a mistake that you made. Every Sunday afternoon, every call, I figure you're on the field for three hours, sometimes maybe a little more, and you're making calls; every little one may make a difference in the game. It might make a difference in a player's record, or score, so with every call you want to be sure that you are exactly 100 percent perfect. The NFL expects the officials to start out being perfect and then get better from there.

There are calls I wish I had … like the Dallas/Philadelphia game, where I blew the whistle too quickly. I made a mistake. It didn't make any effect on the game at the time, but you don't want to do it wrong. You want to do it right. The more times you make the wrong call or make a mistake, you get down-rated—that's what they call it in the NFL. You get a black mark, and the more black marks you get, the less chance you have of working in the playoffs—so you want no black marks at the end of the season.

If you have fewer than other people do, that's how you get to the playoffs and to the Super Bowl. And the records show that there are four Super Bowls that I refereed. Two back-to-back. I was rated the top official that year in my position. Every call you make is important. There is no one call I ever made that decided a game that I felt was wrong. There are some people who may disagree. They thought the call I made was wrong, and that's their opinion.

Doug: All you can do is your best with calls and the information you have got in that moment.

Jim: I think the thing I learned from it is that you've got to develop a strong sense of self. The self-confidence that you know that you're right. You can't be arrogant about it. You can't be pompous about it. You can't be to the point where you aren't going to listen to other opinions, but on that field, you have to have a lot of self-confidence. That was a great thing for me to learn. I started in the NFL when I was thirty; I was one of the youngest officials. And I'm working on the field with players that are almost that age, or even older. This is a major professional sport. This is the biggest thing in the country. I have got to be strong in my opinion and believe in myself. I can't let it bother me that 77,000 people are booing—that they think I'm wrong—or that the coach thinks I am wrong. When you get into some legendary coaches like Vince Lombardi—and he's such a legend—when he disagrees with your call, you've got to believe you're doing the right thing. You've got to prepare yourself and trust that you know what you're doing, that you normally do the right thing.

Doug: This is so crucial. A lot of people when they are trying to get to their goals, they often let coworkers or family members or negative situations get them to question whether they are doing the right thing for themselves or not. What you have said is so important.

Jim: I think it's also important along with that, as you strengthen your self-confidence, is to have some mentors. I have had the best, not only in education but in officiating, to help me. So I've gone to them for advice; I've asked them to evaluate calls; I've listened to their advice. Learned from them and corrected my mistakes, but once you're on the field in front of all those people, it's important that you have the right direction and know what you're doing and believe in yourself and stick to it. We have found in officiating you have got to make decisions quickly. You can't sit down at a board table and take twenty to thirty minutes to decide something. You have got to make a decision quickly. And you've got to be confident. Because if the players or the coaches or the fans see that this guy is not sure what he is doing, they'll get after you.

It'll really disrupt your self-confidence. So you've got to be strong in what you do. At the end of the game, once it's over and you evaluate your performance—and we always evaluate the performance. That's one of the tenets that I had. When I walked off the field after the game, I asked myself, *Did I leave the game better than I found it? Did I do a better job than I hoped to do?* I want to do a good job. But did I do a better job? I evaluated every call; I evaluated everything that I did. I watched myself on film.

And then be very self-critical about the little things. It's the little things that make the difference. If it's not the little things, and the things are really big and major, you shouldn't be there. You haven't done your homework well enough to earn the right to be at that level. But it's the little things; it's tweaking all the time.

In thirty-one years, particularly the last twenty, we have had more and more emphasis on evaluation. I don't think a day went by that I didn't spend time trying to be the best at what I can do. If you take it for granted, you're not going to get there. Players are out there working at it every day. They are trying to get better. They are having coaches teach them new techniques. And you as an individual need to have mentors. You need people you can bounce things off of. "Hey, what about this idea? What about that? What are you doing here?" And be honest with yourself and be willing to accept the criticism.

I always say, accept criticism as a gift. If someone criticizes you in a way that will be helpful, then it's a gift. Look at it that way. Now don't look it at if it's someone trying to tear you down; that's not going to help you, but if you can learn from it, it's helpful. Always be looking for ways to improve. Cavette Roberts used to say, "School is never out for the professional." You are always, always learning. My lifelong goal is learning.

Doug: So what has been the greatest obstacle for you, and how did you overcome it?

Jim: The greatest obstacle, I think, was time. If you look at the time I was a high school principal, Monday through Friday I was in the school building taking care of students, teachers, and parents and the community and the whole thing. Saturday morning I got on an airplane, and on Sunday afternoon I was at a football game for three hours. Now it may only seem like three hours out of the seven days, but those three hours were very, very important pertaining to what was going on at that particular time. And then Sunday night I'd fly back to my school to be there for Monday morning.

If there was one downside to all I did, as my four children were growing up, I was on the football field from August to January. And I didn't get to see them grow up as much as I would have liked to. That's been a downside to me. The time element has just not been there. There is always something going on, even today. Time has always been a factor for me, and I just keep working on it.

Doug: That makes sense. The use of time has a lot to do with how far a person can go toward accomplishing their dreams. And it always seems like there is not enough time. It really does need to be used wisely. If you were coaching an athlete, what do you feel would be the most important things to teach them?

Jim: I think number one would be preparation. You have got to work at it. Preparation is true of any athlete or coach or teacher. You can't just walk into any job and expect it to go well for you.

I think of Larry Bird from the Boston Celtics; he would go out and practice three hours before the games. Shooting, shooting, and shooting, long before the game started. Long before the game starts, you've got to do your homework. You've got to practice and go over and over and over. I think the second thing is to have mentors and teachers to help you learn.

And say, "Whatever I'm doing, can you help me do a better job with that?" And learning from others; don't ever think you have all the answers because no one has all the answers.

Someone told me one time, "Play alone and you'll be alone." And that's the third part: you can't do it by yourself. A team effort is what it is all about. You've got to work with a team. One of the things that I like about sports is that it teaches you, you've got to work with other people.

In English class, history class, in arithmetic, you don't learn teamwork. You don't learn teamwork in the classroom. You learn teamwork on the field. So I've always encouraged my kids to get involved in some kind of a sport. They don't have to be the best. They don't have to be the star. They just have to get involved, because you learn to work with other people.

I have told lots of young people an employer only wants three things from you: (1) Get to work on time. (2) Don't steal from him. (3) Get along with other people. If you can do those three things, you'll always have a job. I think if you do those three things in anything you do, you'll always be successful. No excuses, no exceptions.

Vince Lombardi told me this, and I've practiced it for years: being early. If the meeting starts at two thirty, I'll be there at two fifteen. Because I need to be there; I don't want to be walking in at the last minute. I'm not good enough to be walking in at the last minute and pick up on what's going on. I've got to be there ahead of time. I don't want to be the last one in. I want to be the first one in. Not because I'm better than anybody else, but because I want to be there ready to go. Those are the kinds of things I think help people to become successful.

Doug: What is your definition of success?

Jim: There have been stacks of books written as tall as your body on that subject. Pages and pages and pages. So to come up with a simple definition may not be fair to all the people that have written those books. But I guess for me, if you have prepared yourself and done the best job you could, you can say to yourself, "I did everything I could to do this right," you are successful. And if you do it that way, you will succeed far more than you fail. But you've got to think about the fact there is no such thing as failure. There may be a setback. You might not make it this time.

I often use the story of my grandson, who broke his leg when he was a kid. I had a talk with the orthopedic surgeon, and he said when the bone had healed, it would be stronger than the original bone. I said, "You mean it will be stronger because of failure?" He said, "Sure. The bone is going to be stronger." So if you have a setback, learn from it. And think in terms of growth. And if you can think in terms of learning from failure, you will be successful. That's really what success is: learning from failure.

Take Responsibility to Lead Yourself

Let him that would move a mountain, first move himself.
—Socrates

Mastery of self is the first step toward all great accomplishments.

Most people need to be told what to do. They are waiting for permission to take control of their situation. They stand idly as spectators, watching others achieve greatness and success. They hope that one day someone will take them and lead them to a similar future. Well, here's the news flash: no one is coming. No one will ever come and create your success for you. You will have to take charge of that situation yourself.

If you can't lead yourself to get off the couch and get started, how do expect to be considered a leader in society and have success?

True success must begin with self-leadership.

The good news is that leadership can be learned and developed. Leadership starts with having a clear direction and is followed up by a firm commitment to your goals or principles. When you get committed to your goals and start doing the right things to get there, others will recognize the leader within you.

In a survey I conducted involving more than 1,500 people, one question I asked was: "What has kept most people from leading themselves or others?" The most common answer? People did not know how to get started or what to do. You may also wonder, "What are the steps to take to lead myself?"

Most people involved in this survey felt the problem was a matter of direction. What was the direction for the first step?

Destination precedes direction.

While direction is important, a destination is essential. A leader can only lead someone when they know where they are going. When you know what your final destination will be, you can then understand what direction you need to go. You can't lead others when you yourself are lost.

You've probably heard the saying, "The journey of a thousand miles begins with a single footstep." I've always thought it would be much more valuable to rephrase it this way: "The journey to where you want to go begins with a step in the right direction." If the destination is clear and the steps in the right direction, perhaps it wouldn't be a journey of a thousand miles after all.

When you know your destination, the direction is obvious.

Speed vs. direction

Many people feel that being busy and accomplishing as many tasks in the shortest amount of time is the same as productivity. But unless these tasks are aligned with the ultimate direction in which they wish to go, their work will be in vain.

Religious leader Neal A. Maxwell once asked the question, "What is more important? Velocity or direction? Direction, of course, for who wants to hurry in the wrong direction?" Many people stop progressing when they get discouraged, thinking that they haven't made enough progress toward a goal. They lose patience because they want things to happen more quickly than they appear to be going. Progress doesn't always appear to be going fast when you are in the middle of it.

Top achievers don't worry as much about their speed as they do the direction. When we focus on direction, speed generally takes care of itself. This principle of destination applies to leading self as much as it does to leading groups.

Use of time

The use of your time will be one of the great factors that will determine whether you will achieve your goals or whether you will not. Achievers are awake and working while others are still sleeping, figuratively and literally.

Achievers are aware of their time. They often chart or schedule it to be effective, and they do not squander time. Take a look at your day and determine how yours is spent and what could be done to improve.

Use of free time

Of course, there are times when we need to work and times that some people consider free time. Free time is something that simply doesn't exist. Let me explain: time is never free. How we use our time can be considered a trade. We will always receive a payment from what we do with our time.

The most successful achievers I have worked with have found a way to maximize the use of their time in whatever setting. In their so-called free time, they gain experience, renew important relationships, and even find opportunities to learn. My brother Randy told me of a conversation he had with one of the drivers of former US President Bill Clinton. From the moment Clinton was picked up from the airport, he had a book in his hand and was learning.

I have been impressed by how many of the world's top achievers think the same way. When most people would sit and enjoy the car ride, top achievers are engaged in activities that pay higher dividends.

Be accountable.

One of the important traits of leaders is that they are accountable. Accountability means to measure your productivity with how you are utilizing your time and resources. It also means to plan for progress.

As you lead yourself, you will need to develop ways that you can be accountable to yourself. You will need to be accountable for your time, resources, the giving of your best efforts, and daily activities.

There are many different strategies that can be used to measure your activities. I make reports for myself at the end of each day for the next day.

To me, they are really accomplishment reports or checklists—a list of things that I need to get done that can be marked either complete or incomplete. In this way my activities are clearly measured. Every one of these points on my checklist is measured against my overall goals.

My activities are calculated to yield the greatest results and productivity. By simply writing down my activities, I can see them all at once. This allows me to compare them at a glance and prioritize which activities are going to be the best use of my time.

By doing this, I have found that I am better able to lead myself and I rarely have to ask what's next.

Often throughout the day a situation may arise where I have to add something new to my list or change priorities, but by staying focused on this list, I find that I control my day rather than being controlled by situations that arise during my day.

Exercise—The rule of seven

The timer was about to go off. There were only seconds left until the city would be left in ruins. Could the day be saved?

The hero on a motorcycle raced against a helicopter filled with darkly clad bad guys. Machine-gun fire burst onto the street. The hero dodged the bullets by near misses. He accelerated the motorcycle, leaving the helicopter behind, nearly tripling the local speed limit. The countdown continued. Less than a minute and everything would be ash.

Skidding to a halt, the hero pounced from the motorbike and burst through the plate-glass window.

There in the center of the floor was the bomb. Removing his helmet, he began to investigate the casing.

The timer continued the countdown ... 10 ... 9 ... 8 ...

Would he be able to disarm the bomb in time?

Most likely you've seen a movie with an action sequence similar to this. We all like the challenge and the tension that come with facing such a deadline.

With this scenario in mind, I have developed a strategy that has allowed me to get more done every day. I call it the rule of seven, named after the famous secret agent 007.

Here's how it works: begin by recording seven major things you will accomplish during the day. Commit to work at them until they are done.

With my list of seven, I now introduce the element of risk. I set myself a deadline of 11:00 a.m. to have all of my seven things done. I try to imagine that I am like James Bond and the deadline has real consequences attached to it.

Studies have demonstrated that most people get only between three and five significant things done every day. They let themselves get distracted by outside forces, or they are just not focused to begin with. Their day passes, and the end result is that just three to five things are complete. The rule of seven has helped me to get things done and stay focused. Often because my first seven things are done by 11:00 a.m., I can add another seven things and have fourteen things done by the day's end. That gives me the benefit of more than three times what an average person does. And it all comes down to the power of focus and deadlines.

Rewards of self-leadership

Self-leadership will become its own reward. You will find increased self-confidence and increased productivity. Often those rewards are not easily seen until you sit still and carefully contemplate all that has happened since your journey began.

Exercise—Reward yourself for a task well done.

One of the most motivating things is to see and feel as though progress is happening. A method to continually recognize your progress is to issue rewards according to a schedule you create for yourself.

The rewards need not be extravagant, but they are a recognition and reminder that things are moving forward.

Include others in these recognitions. Showing appreciation is important because you will need their support as well in your journey to success.

Exercise—What is the ideal employee?

Describe to me the ideal employee you would like to have working for you. What is his or her work ethic like? How often will he or she take breaks?

What obstacles will overwhelm him or her? How hard will he or she try to get a task completed? What tasks can he or she be trusted with?

Now consider for a moment, in the context of self-leadership, that this employee is you. Are you satisfied with your current efforts as your own employer? What would need to happen to make you more effective?

Take responsibility to lead yourself—Questions to consider

- What is the direction I am currently going?
- Where do I want to go as a leader?
- How am I using my free time?
- What activities are currently distracting me from leading myself better?
- If I were an employee to my, what changes would I require?
- How am I using my time?
- How am I using my free time?
- How will I measure my accountability?
- How is my time being spent when it is time to work?
- What rewards will I give to myself?

Vision, Belief, and Faith

Never underestimate the power of dreams
and the influence of the human spirit.
We are all the same in this notion:
The potential for greatness lives within each of us.
——Wilma Rudolph

Vision

Vision is about your point of view. It is more about what you see as possible than what you see in existence. Your ability to see the invisible will have a direct link to what will be possible in your life.

If you can't see it, you will never be able to believe it's possible; if you don't believe it, you'll never be able to do it.

What you see as possible is the beginning of all things that appear in your reality. One of the greatest assets that all successful people have is the ability to see possibility where others see only the impossible.

How big is your vision?

Are you able to see beyond what lies immediately before you? Do you have a grand vision that will lead you to stretch further than ever before?

Your vision of what is possible has the greatest effect on what the end result will look like.

If we think small, we do small things.
If we think big, we begin to do big things.

There is a story that is told of a press conference the opening day of Disney World in Orlando. Walt Disney never lived to see the Orlando theme park completed. During the press conference, a reporter commented to Roy Disney, Walt's brother, that "it's too bad that Walt never got a chance to see the finished park." Roy's statement back to the reporter was that "If Walt hadn't seen it first, the rest of us would never have had the chance to see it either."

We need to secure a clear vision of what we want our future to look like. It needs to be big enough to make us stretch, but not so big that it paralyzes us. You'll know the difference because when something is just big enough, it feels right and you will be able to get started right away.

Belief

Belief is the level of commitment in the mind as to the likelihood or probability of a thing coming to pass.

Belief is at the foundation of achievement. Before you can desire to have changes in your life, you must believe they are possible. *Belief always precedes the fire of desire.* Desire always precedes creation of the reality. Very rarely are marvelous things accomplished by accident.

Your belief is the single most important thing you can take with you as you pursue a goal. When you don't believe something is possible, your vision to see the impossible is diminished.

You Can

If you believe you can, you can.
If you think you are beaten, you are.
If you think you dare not, you don't.
If you want to win but think you can't,
It's almost a cinch you won't.

If you think you'll lose, you've lost.
For out in the world we find
That success begins with a fellow's will;
It's all in the state of mind.

Life's battles don't always go
To the stronger faster man;
But sooner or later the man who wins
Is the one who thinks he can.

—Unknown

Vision isn't just what you see.

I learned a very important thing in regard to vision and belief from a family member of mine. My uncle Danny has developed quite a reputation as a horse trainer. In fact, he has been so successful that many people have sought him out when difficult circumstances have arisen with their horses. Such an experience took place a few years ago.

A rancher just outside a town called Stettler, Alberta, hired my uncle to work with one of his more difficult horses.

Early one morning my uncle went out and began to prepare the horse for the day's work. As he began to brush the horse, he stepped behind the animal, and that's when things went bad.

Suddenly and without warning the horse was spooked and kicked both its back legs out in the direction of my uncle. Without time to move, he was kicked directly in the face with both hoofs.

My uncle fell motionless to the floor. Others nearby rushed to his side to keep the horse from trampling him further. Things did not look good.

Immediately the EMS was called, and they arrived moments later by helicopter. They took my uncle to a hospital in the city of Calgary. As he arrived, they began to connect him to machines that would preserve his life. It was at about this time that our family got a call to come to the hospital as quickly as possible. It was a seriously critical situation.

When we arrived, the doctor suggested that my uncle, who was now in a coma, would probably live. But he might suffer brain damage, and he would certainly be blind. Our family prayed. Things did not change that day. In fact, they did not change for quite some time.

When my uncle came out of the coma, he did not have brain damage, but he was blind and would be for the rest of his life.

My uncle returned to a world built mostly for people who had sight.

There were many challenges for him as he had to learn everything all over again. Some of the lessons were harder and more painful than others—such as lessons that involved hot stoves, stairs, and even crossing a busy street. All the things that we take for granted.

One day my uncle and I were sitting on his front step, and he leaned over to me and said something quite profound.

He said that after all of the experiences he had been through and with everything that he had to relearn, there was one lesson he never had before. That new lesson was the most powerful lesson he had ever learned. Pointing to his eyes he said, "Vision is not about what you see." Then pointing to his heart he said, "Vision is about what you believe."

Vision is not just what you see; vision is about what you believe. It was one of the most profound things I had ever heard. What is your vision for your success? The vision you choose to believe will have a profound effect on your ability to be successful in the future.

Faith

Faith is the outward demonstration of an inward belief. Faith is the first step into the darkness when the answers aren't yet clear. All great accomplishments have been acts of faith. These acts of faith have required sacrifice, commitment, and perseverance before all of the answers have arrived.

Faith and doubt cannot exist at the same time. When we doubt our abilities, our efforts are not in faith. They are only partial efforts. Success requires a total commitment. When we doubt, we hold back part of ourselves. Reserved efforts create a climate where failure is imminent.

Sacrifice is an important word. No incredible success has come without sacrifice. When you prioritize your activities to get to a goal, there will be some things that you will have to let go of. What are you willing to give up to bring about your success? When your commitment is equal to the achievement, you will be able to accomplish it.

Exercise—Belief, Faith, and Vision

Consider carefully a situation in your life right now. What do you really believe the outcome will be? Why do you think it will be that way? Do you believe that the end result awaits you, or do you feel that it may be elusive and difficult to grasp?

What roadblocks are keeping you from believing wholeheartedly in the final victory of accomplishing this goal?

Identifying the roadblocks can be easy if we invest the time to think about it. Most people become so paralyzed looking at the roadblocks that they never break through them.

> Our minds are wired to see the dangers, obstacles, and challenges more quickly than we see the opportunities.

Exercise—Eliminate fears and roadblocks.

Take a sheet of paper and fold it in half vertically. On one side make a list of the things that are causing you to doubt. Express them clearly and leave nothing out.

In column two, write clearly how you will cancel out those objections.

On the back of the paper include past experiences where you have had the courage to beat similar obstacles and doubts. Describe events where you have proven to yourself that you can do difficult things like those on your list. Be sure to spend far more time on the courageous elements than the doubtful expressions. Often while doing this exercise, I like to listen to inspiring music.

When we look carefully at the incredible things we have done and the courageous things we are capable of, we begin to see we are stronger than the doubtful opposition.

Exercise—Goal journal

Keeping a goal journal is another brilliant way to keep focused on victories and establish a strong belief in yourself. I have a personal section in my journal I call the Victory Pages. Within that part of my goal journal, I have pasted newspaper clippings, reviews, testimonials, and photographs of times when I was courageous or made a real difference for someone. Reviewing those pages, especially when I have challenges and doubt, has made an incredible difference for me.

Vision, Belief, and Faith—Questions to consider

- What do I see?
- What do I believe about it?
- What will I sacrifice for it?
- What do I genuinely belief is possible for me?
- What do I want to do that I have previously believed impossible?
- Do I believe that my vision of success is something I can really attain?
- Do I have the faith to proceed, even without all the answers?
- What does my vision of success look like?
- Is it big enough?

Excerpts from the Success Interviews: Anthony Daniels

From his earliest memory, Anthony wanted to be a professional actor. He experienced moderate successes in the theater, and then an opportunity appeared that changed his future forever. He met George Lucas.

After this meeting, Anthony was invited to participate in a little movie that few people believed in called *Star Wars*.

It was revolutionary and tried to break every rule imaginable. But because of George Lucas's belief in the project and his perseverance, it turned out to be the greatest science fiction film ever made.

Anthony is the only actor to ever appear in all of the *Star Wars* films (*Star Wars, The Empire Strikes Back, The Return of the Jedi, The Phantom Menace, Attack of the Clones, The Revenge of the Sith*, and the latest installment, *The Clone Wars*), as the golden protocol droid C3PO.

Anthony has been involved in many of the *Star Wars* spin-offs. Some of the more memorable include performing in three radio dramatizations, tap dancing on the *Muppet Show*, dancing with Donny and Marie Osmond, taking part in the Oscar ceremonies, befriending Big Bird on *Sesame Street*, voicing the animated figure in Disney's Star Tours ride, becoming a breakfast cereal—Kellogg's C-3POs, conducting the London Symphony and the Boston Pops Orchestra, and starring in the cartoon series *Droids*. Currently he is working on the animated TV series *Clone Wars*.

Doug: Hi, Anthony. It's great to chat with you. You've had an incredible journey appearing in all of the *Star Wars* movies as C3P0. But let's start at the beginning. When did you first realize that you wanted to be an actor?

Anthony: Well, I don't remember a time I didn't want to be an actor. Well, I suppose if I thought back, there was a time I wanted to be a milk delivery person at one point, but I was probably about five. And I think after that there was something about the magic of the theater that made me want to be an actor. I don't remember ever having a serious thought otherwise.

Doug: Your parents had other plans for you. Let's talk about that for a minute.

Anthony: Well, back when I was eighteen, which would be around 1964 or 63, it was a very different world then. Back then a real career was the thing you went for. So a real career back then was a teacher or a doctor or a lawyer; an engineer, a scientist, a banker would be good. Makes you laugh now, doesn't it? And this is what you would call a profession. Acting was also called a profession, but with a slightly wry smile. So my parents really wanted me to have a safe, secure profession.

Doug: They wanted you to be a lawyer, didn't they?

Anthony: When I said I wanted to be an actor, they sort of said, "Well, why don't you be a lawyer?" I lost all enthusiasm and just sort of said, "Okay." And I tried it and was intensely unhappy. The one thing that kept me going was to be in amateur plays and productions. You know, evenings and weekends. And that was what I lived for. Of course, many people have jobs where their real pleasure time is their leisure time, but when you are heavily at odds with a job you want to do, life is pretty miserable.

Doug: The key is to find your passion first and the job second.

Anthony: I was lucky I had a passion. Some people don't have it. You can call it a vocation or a calling or whatever you like. But some people are just happy with any old job. Somebody with a calling really needs to do that job; there's nothing silly about it, it's the real thing. You can have a calling to do the weirdest stuff. I mean acting is pretty weird. You know, some people have a calling to be a foot doctor; you know, of course, that I would run a mile from that. But thank goodness there are people who are foot doctors in this world. I think you'd have to have a calling to be able to put up with being a foot doctor—don't know about you—so I guess I had a calling and a need, and eventually I was incredibly lucky.

My grandmother died and left me a small amount of money, and that enabled me to have a slightly freer attitude. The real reason I felt able to be an actor was that during one of these amateur evenings or weekends, a man who was a member of the same acting society heard me say, "I wish I was an actor." And he looked at me—he was a teacher—and he said, "If you want to be an actor, be an actor." And he was the first person to unlock the idea in me that I was a free agent. I could do something I wanted to do. And some months later, I got myself into drama school.

Doug: That's fantastic. It must have been comforting to know that you now had someone who believed in you and supported your dream. It sounds like there were a lot of people who preferred you found a profession. There were lots of obstacles in the way. How did you keep going now that you decided this is what you wanted to do?

Anthony: Well, I suppose it was that I believed there was nothing else I wanted to live for. Which sounds maybe exaggerated. But you know, I could do all sorts of other jobs. I could stack the shelves in the supermarket. But it wouldn't have given me the quality of life to make my life worth living. And again, I think if somebody has a calling, that is what they must do. I had to do it. And of course, you were absolutely right, things got in the way that made this given profession difficult. Acting is very hard to choose as a profession. But my belief was that this was the only thing that gave me any sort of satisfaction, any kind of sense of fulfillment.

You know, people get fulfilled in all sorts of different ways, and mine was the need to talk to and be with an audience, an audience of any size. Just to be able to perform. So sometimes it's very hard to explain, and a lot of this comes from inside. When you try to explain it, it can sometimes sound silly and ridiculous and so on.

Doug: So when did you start to realize that acting was going to be your career? When did you start to see these dreams develop and begin to experience success?

Anthony: I was very, very lucky. It was at a three-year course at a college. I had a teacher—another inspirational teacher. This time he was in the sound department, and we used to make recordings and readings and so on. And every year the BBC in London would have a competition for all the schools across the country, and they choose one student out of maybe a hundred and something to be the prizewinner. And I was the prizewinner. With the title of BBC award winner, and also more important then—it doesn't happen now—it gave me a union ticket, which meant I could be a member of British Equity, the actors' union. It's all changed now. But back then you couldn't get a job unless you had an Equity membership, and you couldn't get an Equity membership without having a job. What a ridiculous catch-22 situation! That's all changed now. But that was the first real victory. I remember being stunned and overwhelmed by it. Then I just got on with it, and for the next six months, I did two big plays a week for the radio. Because we still have a large radio drama audience in Britain.

I learned a lot about voice production from the radio. After that I began to get roles in other plays in theaters. And on the last night of one of these productions, a man came up to me and said that I was pretty good. You know, people say things in theater and you don't always believe them, but I found out who he was. He ran a very successful part of the National Theater. I went in on Monday and signed in on the labor exchange, where when you have no work, you go and sign your name and they give you a small amount of money each week, and then Tuesday the phone rang, and it was my agent saying, "They want you to go and join the national company."

So I think the next day, the Wednesday, I went and joined the National Theatre. I was there for two years. It was during that time that my agent came up with the name George Lucas.

Doug: Who's he? (laughing)

Anthony: Who's he? Back in 1975 he wanted to make apparently a low-budget sci-fi movie. I wasn't really interested in sci-fi.

Doug: Is it true that you actually asked for a refund on a movie ticket you purchased for *2001: A Space Odyssey*?

Anthony: It's 100 percent true. I kind of smile at myself for having the courage to do that. It was about a third of the way through the movie. I did go to the manager, who was wearing a tux and a little dickey bow tie and that kind of thing. He was quite tall. And he looked down at me and said, "Why do you want your money back?" And I said, "Because it's a really boring film." And he said, "Get lost." He was so rude to me.

Nowadays, no one would ever speak to you in such a rude way, but he did. And of course, I was to eat my words. Because when I did eventually meet George Lucas, we talked about *2001*, and I ended up watching it again, by myself in the Fox screening room. And indeed, flying to America the other day, I watched it again on the airplane. I was amazed. There it was again. And now I'm very fond of it.

Doug: So tell me about how you got involved with *Star Wars*.

Anthony: Well, my agent explained that this American wanted someone to play the role of a robot, and she could sense my negativity instantly. Because she said, "No, no, I think you should go and see him." And I said no.

I didn't want to play a robot. Because back then, it was nothing. A robot was a Darlek, you know, from the *Dr. Who* series. Darleks look a bit like R2D2, but now they can go upstairs, fly, and do everything. Just like R2D2 can. In the old days, Darleks were men huddled over a bicycle kind of arrangement. They were sort of wobbling wheels in a box.

Doug: And prior to R2D2 and C3P0, most robots didn't have much for personalities.

Anthony: They were dead lumps of metal. So why would I do this? And my agent actually said, "Don't be so …" Well, she used a really vulgar expression, and she was an agent and they are tough people. She told me, "Don't be so stupid," and said, "Go meet him; you never know what it could lead to." So I went.

And famously I walked into his office, and there was a perfectly ordinary, downbeat, sort of quiet, shy man. And he spoke with an American accent. And he wore jeans and the same plaid shirt he even wears to this day, and then we had a very feeble conversation. Neither of us was terribly enthusiastic. He had seen an actor every five minutes of the day. I think I was number 321 of that particular session. He had had actors up to his ears. And the thing that really sold it to me, the movie, was the artist's impression on the wall. What you call the concept paintings, where somebody drafts out some visual ideas for the movie.

I didn't know any words like Death Star or Darth Vader or anything like that. But there amongst these pictures was this strange metal character staring out of the frame towards me. And somehow we connected. There was a complete communion of spirits. I cannot explain it to this day. It's never happened before or since. I connected with the picture. The face in the picture was saying, "Come and join me." It wanted to connect. It was neither male nor female. It was just made of metal.

And so I kind of went away a bit stunned; about an hour, I'd been there, I think. So there was a whole lineup of people outside by now. And then they sent a script the next day. It's tough enough to understand what *Star Wars* is about when you see the movie, but when you read it page by page, scene by scene, POV by POV [point of view by point of view], it's very tough reading. The one thing I got was that every time this metal man came in, he had a weird take on everything. He was different. He wasn't a hero; he wasn't a villain. He was just himself.

So the next day, I literally went back to meet George, and after an hour of talking sci-fi and stuff, there was a pause, and I asked, "May I play the part?" And he just said, "Sure." The way he says yes is "sure." And there we are; that was the beginning of it all.

Doug: What was your most challenging part of working on the *Star Wars* **movies?**

Anthony: The first challenge was to make the suit around my body. So the first hurdle was to get a mold around my body, and creating that was really quite a bizarre experience. And not entirely comfortable. The second was to be there while the art crew made the suit. They needed me to be there every second day while I was still doing another show in the theater during the evening. So that was a challenge. But being out there in the desert and putting on that suit for the first time, when it wasn't in fact finished. It didn't work. It was hugely uncomfortable because it didn't fit together. And it pinched me and scraped and everything. Then the challenge came to, *how do I really get a personality through this metal and plastic?* Somehow my training did it. We'll come onto the voice maybe later.

So I had individual challenges to be the person in the script. I interpreted the words the way I saw them. They weren't my words. I was given the lines to speak, and I said them my way. And I tried to make the best of it. This was a new departure for me. This was a challenge I had never had before. I played a parrot on the radio, but hey, that's not difficult.

Doug: There was no one that had ever done what you were doing before. There was no reference material or previous examples to consider. You were inventing something brand-new.

Anthony: Yes, That was the way George was approaching the movie, to create something brand-new. Kind of old-fashioned, but brand-new. One of the really huge challenges was, in the script I had read R2D2 would blurp a response or bleep a reply. The real shock to me was that R2D2 was totally silent throughout. So that in some of the longer scenes, I was carrying what should have been pages of dialogue as pages of monologue. And sometimes in desperation, I would write his lines, or my interpretation of his lines. So that I would learn the whole page. It would make it easier for me to know that he was saying, "I am going over there." And I would say, "What do you mean? Where are you going?" Because I had to make it real for myself. So here I am wearing this metal suit and I am best friends with a box that runs over my feet or tries to push me over. Sometimes there was an actor named Kenny Baker inside to make it wobble. But other times, pretty much every time it moved, it was pulled on a string or a remote control gizmo operated by the camera and really quite uncontrollable.

And the object itself was really heavy; it had lots of batteries inside it and radio receivers and that kind of thing. And it used to crash into me, and once I really had to stop it from falling down into Luke Skywalker's home. There were some steps there, and it really was going to crash and burn. It nearly knocked me over. All that kind of thing. But the big thing was trying to create a relationship with a garbage bin. And at one point I did ask George if he could do a beep or something when I had finished my line so it would make it a dialogue rather than a monologue. And he tried it—it was terrible. So I just improvised the scene, all the scenes that R2D2 was in, and made it look like I believed in him, and therefore the audience believed.

Doug: You did an incredible job. How did you come up with the voice? I understand that at one point they were interested to cast you in the suit, but had other plans for the voice.

Anthony: That's right. I had tried over six months so many different voices. I can't tell you. And I didn't like any of them. I didn't tell anyone else. It was embarrassing sometimes. That's something you have to get over as an actor—getting embarrassed. I don't know. I worked and worked and worked. And I bored myself senseless.

As the day approached, I still hadn't made a decision. And then out there in the desert, dressed up, being Threepio, a number of voices came together, a number of ideas from the script came together, a number of ideas about the situation came together, and Threepio arrived. George Lucas had written a very clever thing into the script about the personality. He had made an android for protocol and etiquette—etiquette sort of being the ultimate way of being polite. And protocol about who should go through a door first, which is the order of magnificence if you like. And this politeness thing was so totally out of place with the whole world that *Star Wars* was, all these explosions and things. So he very cleverly made this dramatic dissonance. Threepio was not happy. He wanted to be somewhere else selling cocktails under a canopy and that sort of thing.

I had a little microphone up by my eyebrow, and then a cable ran over and down my back to a radio transmitter shoved in a very tight area. So they would get a really bad guide track. And I sounded really much more like Darth Vader. They would use that. And often I would rerecord it immediately on set to give the editors a clear track. I could remember my timing and so on. And then yes, some six months later, I went over to Hollywood to put my voice on it. And it was then that I found out that George had tried people like Richard Dreyfuss to put his voice, his character, on the film. George explained, and I was a little surprised and never thought of Threepio being this kind of uptight British butler. And you know, with an actor, unless you direct them a certain way, they will do their own thing. And George was directing the whole movie, so he didn't have time to tell me how to play my part or anything. He was busy making sure that something got on film before the whole budget crashed and destroyed his project for sure. You know he was dealing with storms that were wrecking the sets, special effects that just did not work, dealing with money problems and Fox Studios.

He actually said the words, "We can fix the voice later." What I didn't realize was that he had originally planning to put another a different voice on. But he was great.

Now here's the thing—talk about challenges. George had taken his script around for many months, I think several years, to many studios and said, "I have this idea for a space movie." And they said, "Get lost, it's rubbish, nobody will ever like it." But he toughed it out. He just believed in it so much that eventually somebody gave him a tiny budget. Twentieth Century Fox, they gave him the seed money, just like my grandmother gave me the seed money to go to drama school. So George got a tiny budget from Fox and made all sorts of compromises in the deal just to get the film done. George is a fine example of sticking to your aim or your goal.

Doug: I think so. I think that it is really important to know that so much can be accomplished when you really believe in something. George Lucas is an incredible example of that.

Anthony: There are plenty of people around who, for whatever reason, can be fairly negative. "No, don't do that; you'll fail. Don't do that; you'll be poor. No, don't do that; you'll be hungry, you'll be unhappy' Don't do that because I tried it and I failed." The human spirit is huge and wonderful and often keeps us alive in times when there doesn't seem to be much point. The need to be alive is very strong, and the need to succeed at something, to move forward, to be adventurous can also be very strong. But it tends to get crushed in people. It's very difficult as an older person or a teacher. You may want to stop someone from doing something that may potentially harm them. And you should, if you see someone standing on the edge of a cliff, you should say to them, "I wouldn't go any farther because it might crumble." Now you may sound like an old maid saying that, but if it crumbles and the guy falls in, wouldn't you wish you had said it? But then if you said it, it might stop somebody from falling off a cliff and learning how to fly. That's a hard point. I wouldn't put George and me in the same boat because he's utterly inspirational. But we share that we went on in spite of people saying nay.

Doug: After *Star Wars* **came out, I understand that all the media campaigns tried to promote R2D2 and C3P0 as actual robots, and I heard that you were having second thoughts about coming back for** *The Empire Strikes Back* **because of that.**

Anthony: It was a very difficult time to be honest. I had a very tough time filming, but that's what filming and role building is about. You have a tough time. But then when you have done it, actors get acknowledged for what they did. Like an artist when he signs his name to a painting. And I fairly quickly realized that nobody was allowed to interview me and my name never appeared on publicity stills. They would say "Luke Skywalker (Mark Hamill) and C3P0 from *Star Wars*."

And it was awhile before I challenged them. They said, "We need people to think that you are a real robot." Well, that was quite difficult. There was no way I was going to spoil people's feelings. It would be like telling them Santa Claus is maybe a myth. I'm still not sure about that. But that was a postfilming challenge. And certainly it took some thought before I agreed to do the second film.

Doug: We're all glad that you did. As a child I remember believing that you were a real robot. It's quite a testament to the skill you had in portraying that character.

Anthony: You know, Doug, that's a really nice sentiment. Thank you. But if you hadn't, then I would have been failing at my job. My job was to be a robot. Nowadays, you will notice that people are much better at giving credit because many more films are created with special effects and remodeled in some way. But now there is an acknowledgement that an actor plays this. And the added video extras on your DVD will show you the whole process.

I think it's fairly simplistic to think the audience is too glim to not accept a film just because they know how it is done. I mean, there are two sides to a film. You can enjoy the whole magic of seeing it from beginning to end and believe all the characters. Then you can enjoy it again by seeing how it was done. So I think times have changed in these thirty or some odd years. I am the only person to be in all six *Star Wars* films.

Doug: That's right. And when we first saw C3P0, there was no such thing as the CG animation that we see today. I mean, George Lucas pioneered so much of this technology. What are the significant changes in playing C3P0 today?

Anthony: Playing him is absolutely no different. He is what he is. He's always been this machine. This domestic appliance if you'd like. He very much depends on the circumstances in which he is put because his personality is set. Your washing machine isn't suddenly going to turn into a refrigerator.

As far as filming now goes, it's almost an extension now of R2D2 not making any sound. In the old films you had these wonderful set pieces that were just magical to look at and touch and play with because it was so beautifully made by the scenic department.

Nowadays, as many people know, the only thing that is in a scene that is real is the floor—whatever the floor is, tile or a rocky surface or whatever. They have to make that real because the floor is the most difficult thing to do in animation, because you need the weight of the character on the floor. But apart from that, about a hundred yards away, there is a green or a blue wall. And you have to imagine.

And if there are monsters, George says in the script that the door opens and whatever he creates flies out. And I say to George, "Well, what do the creatures look like? Are they big or are they little? Do they fly?" And he says, "Kind of this big." And that helps because I am looking at the place which will later be animated.

You need to use your imagination. It's like going back to the days when I was on radio. On radio you don't have sets, and you only have a microphone. The thing is, that's not so much fun. You can't walk onto a set and say, "My gosh, look at that. Isn't that incredible?"

You can say that when you see the movie because the artists will have put that all in during CG and postproduction. So now R2D2 still does not talk to me, but often in the scenes he wasn't there at all. Because George would put him in digitally later on. Again, sometimes it's just easier to put him in afterward.

So my last shot in the *Star Wars* movies was by myself on a blue carpet with a blue background talking to R2D2, who would be put in later. So I hauled along a vacuum cleaner as a chum during the rehearsal. The crew liked it.

Doug: How funny.

Anthony: George didn't leave it in the movie. Which is sad. So a lot of it is in my head. So when I go and see the films, it's really quite interesting to see. And what is glorious is that for the most part, it is seamless. And one of the things I like about the other film I am in, so I'll actually be in all seven *Star Wars* films now, *Clone Wars*—the thing I like is that it is all digital. Beautifully painted, beautifully rendered. The lighting is superb. It is filmed like a movie would be. And because everything is CG, there is a completeness about it. Nothing jars.

Doug: I enjoyed it. So, Anthony, what are you up to next?

Anthony: More *Clone Wars*. Next week I'll be back in England. Right now I am a visiting professor, as they call me, at Carnegie Mellon University, the Entertainment Technology Center, where I come several times a year and tutor the postgraduate students in various things around entertainment and the use of technology in entertainment. I find that so enlivening. Because they are all twenty something-year-olds and all very clever with computers. Also, because of my various work around academia, I am working with the Boston Science Museum in an exhibition called "*Star Wars*—Where Science Meets Imagination."

I've been lucky enough to work with real robotists and real scientists who know the real side of this. And I really floored them one day. There was this big conference and I gave a speech and I said, "Do you realize that for all the clever stuff you do with computers and robots, I am the only person in this whole hall who knows what it feels like to be a machine?" And there was this tremendous silence. Being involved in this has certainly given me a new perspective in my life.

Actually, here's another little step in life I never thought of. Because of my work, I met the dean of this part of the university, who eventually got in touch and said, "I want you to come and teach the students." And I said, "No, what could I teach?" "You can teach them; I know you can." And I'm going, "No, no, no." Well, the result is about four years ago, I started coming here, and they still ask me back so it means that somebody again had to encourage me to believe in myself. I would have liked to believe I could teach. But I didn't think so. And now I know to some extent I can. And that's a great feeling.

So listen to people who believe in you. It's very easy not to believe in yourself sometimes, and sometimes there are people around you that are helpful and let you believe in yourself. I have been very lucky to meet one or two in my life. There's not many around.

Doug: This is something important that we want to share with our audience, the importance of finding people that do believe in you and discovering what you are capable of. Throughout your career, you have been surrounded by some incredible people. What attributes do you think they have in common?

Anthony: I think probably determination. You know you don't have to be rude and ugly and sort of forceful; you just have to carry on believing in spite of all the things that get in your way. Believing that you can do it. Not that you're right, just that you can do it. People that think they are right all the time become a bit of a pain. We were talking about people who tell you you can't do things, but try it at least. What's the worst that could happen? If you never try, you'll never know what might have been.

Doug: And you may pass by something that changes your life for the positive forever.

Anthony: I couldn't help noticing the other day that my parents would have preferred me to be a banker back in 1964. On the news this week banking has ceased to be the safe career that it once was, and these days one of the groups of students that I teach here are video game makers.

Gaming now has an industry greater than the film industry and greater than television and any other form of electronic entertainment. Gaming is a huge industry. Who would have thought back in 1964 that somebody who made games for people would have a good career? The world is changing all the time. People make money doing all sorts of strange things. And that's okay. Think, as they say, outside the box.

Also, I do get fed up of meeting young people who, when you say, "What do you want to do?" they say, "I want to be rich and famous." That's a silly thing to say. Think of something you want to do, and if you can make money at it, you're very lucky. But if you want to do it, you'll be very happy anyway. We don't need that much money. We don't need two or three cars. The home stuff that advertising tells you you need for a happy life … I shouldn't say this, but how many versions of the iPod do we need to achieve happiness? We don't need all this stuff. And if you don't need it, you don't need the money to buy it. Be happy in your choices in life, and that will go a long way.

Doug: Thanks, Anthony. It's been great chatting with you again. We shared a lot of valuable thoughts that I think are worth thinking about.

Anthony: This has been my experience. My personal experience. And that's the way I see it. I don't really have wisdom. I have experience to share. And if it tweaks one person into thinking, *what the heck, I am going to do that thing*—providing it doesn't hurt anyone else and it doesn't hurt you, then risk it. But don't tell your parents I said that.

Doug: Thanks, Anthony.

Anthony: Thanks, Doug. So I guess you have to say, if you think with strength, then the force will be with you.

Be Teachable

If we feel we can't learn, we will remain the same
while the world around us will continue to grow.

Knowledge is a curious thing. The world we live in is moving at an ever-accelerating pace. It has been said that by the time a computer program reaches the marketplace, it is already two to three years out-of-date.

When a person graduates from university with a degree, he or she can be as much as five years behind what is required to be competitive. Most of what people learn in order to be successful in the real world comes from their peers, who are currently involved in the marketplace and currently creating positive results.

Don't just get advice—get the best advice.

It is well worth mentioning that most top achievers I studied get their information from the top 10 percent in the industry they are involved in. If they are going to invest, they invest with the best. If they are seeking a business consultant, they get one of the best. If they are taking golf lessons, they get the best. They don't have time to spend learning average things. They want the best.

How quickly can you apply what you learn?

While learning is important, the essential question is "How fast can you apply the information you are learning?" The most successful people are those who can assimilate information quickly and implement it immediately into their daily activities.

It has been said that life is like trying to run up an escalator the wrong way. If you run faster than the steps coming toward you, you will eventually get to the top. If you do only what is required, you will stand still. But if you are satisfied to do nothing, you will very soon find yourself at the bottom.

People who feel that they know it all and have all of the answers are quickly left behind and are frequently replaced by someone more capable and competent. Constant change is what allows more room for tomorrow's achievers. One of the sure ways to become successful is to stay teachable and seek out learning wherever you can.

All the skills that you will ever need in this life are learnable. Other people are using them, and so can you. It is not a matter of talent as much as it is a willingness to learn and to be determined.

Not too long ago I had a chance to sit and chat with Clay Kaytis, who works as a top animator for Walt Disney Studios. Clay did not start there.

In fact, by his own admission, he wasn't even the greatest artist. He started in a much lower position, and through learning the skills that make great animators, he progressed over time. "It took me fifteen years to get here. I started at the bottom. And I wasn't the most talented artist. In fact, you don't have to be the most talented to succeed. But you do have to be willing to learn and keep getting better. It is really a matter of determination."

Willingness to learn unlocks the doors of possibility faster than any other key.

Once you understand a law or principle, you can apply it to create different results in your life.

Consider the example of the Wright brothers, who upon understanding the basic principles of flight, were able to fly their historic flight at Kitty Hawk. And those who followed them were able to utilize all the knowledge from that point to the present to create supersonic jets and even spacecraft that now explore other worlds.

If we can draw upon the lessons and teachings of others, we can speed our progression to our end results. We will go further, faster, and more far-reachingly than ever before.

Learning and Experience

All great things come to those who are prepared to learn. Malcolm Gladwell in his fascinating book *Outliers* makes the observation that people cannot be top experts in any field until they have invested at least ten thousand hours of practice. These are hours of learning and refinement of a skill, developing it to the level of master. If it takes you ten thousand hours to become an expert, why is it that so many people give up after just one or two tries? No wonder they are not seeing great successes in their lives. We have got to be willing to pay the price in terms of practice, performance, and learning the skill.

A recent study demonstrated that you don't necessarily need to invest ten thousand hours to make a difference. Much can be learned in a small amount of regular study time each day. An hour of committed study daily will place you in the top 10 percent of those in your profession.

Carefully consider what you can add to your learning tools in terms of books, DVDs, seminars, and one-on-one interactions with people who can teach you and guide you to understand the things that will make a significant difference for you.

It is not uncommon for the average person today to have many full-time jobs through the course of his or her working career. One report I recently read said the average number of jobs could be as high as fourteen. The report went on to say that most people will rarely work long-term or full-term for a company, but will work in short stints with multiple companies. Many at some time will become self-employed.

This is another reason why it is so important that you become trained in a set of skills that will make you valuable in a variety of circumstances.

Exercise—What would I like to learn?

I have had a chance to meet some pretty incredible people in my life. I have spent time with business leaders who have created billion-dollar brands, celebrities who have won Academy Awards, and musicians who have won the music-industry equivalents. I have spent time with Olympians and professional players from major athletic clubs. One significant lesson I have learned is that when I get to spend time with these people, time is valuable. To be effective I need to plan in advance what I want to learn when I am with them. When I plan what I want to learn, my learning is accelerated.

I will sometimes make a list of questions I am seeking answers to or even problems I need to solve that they may be able to help with. And in the course of our interactions, I will address these with them.

Success doesn't just rub off by being around successful people. You have got to have an intention.

As a side benefit, because I am prepared, they often give me all the time I need. They know I value my time and theirs as well.

Now you don't need one of the world's top achievers nearby to implement this strategy. Pull out the business cards you collected at the last event you attended. Look through these contacts. Who could teach you the lessons you need?

Chances are good, even in that stack of business cards, you have contacts who can add some great lessons to your pool of experience. Write down a plan of what you would like to learn and then get them on the phone.

Be teachable—Questions to consider

- What is the most important skill that I could learn that would go toward accomplishing my goal?
- Where would I learn it?
- Who around me could become a great teacher to me?
- What am I really investing to learn this skill?
- What more could I do?
- Who in my circle of associates can I learn from?
- What will I specifically try to learn from them?
- What have I learned that can help me get to my goal?
- What have I learned that is not helping me?
- Where can I learn more of what will work?

Ask Appropriate Questions

What you ask for determines in a large measure what you will get.

Questions are one of our most powerful tools for getting on the right track toward achievement.

Without asking what is working and why not, we will often keep trying the same things without experiencing a change in results. Some of the most successful people in the world have simply gotten there because they learned how to ask the right questions.

In this book you'll notice I conclude every chapter with questions to consider. Please do not dismiss them. In fact, I believe that your success will be a reflection of the quality of your answers.

Often just spending time considering the answers to these questions can save you incredible amounts of time and provide greater clarity in understanding what it is you are really trying to achieve.

When we probe and explore the questions of why, what, when, where, how, and even who, we are like the doctor who is able to get past the symptoms and really get down to the issues at hand. When those issues are discovered, the answers on how to treat those issues most often appear very quickly.

Asking deep probing questions can often feel uncomfortable, sometimes even embarrassing or frustrating. It is so much easier to answer again and again, "I don't know."

Top achievers carefully ask questions that will lead deeper and deeper into a matter. Clarity is the beginning of success.

Exercise—Ask appropriate questions.

Take a current issue or concern that you are grappling with and write it in the center of a blank piece of paper. Now around that sentence begin to brainstorm. It is best to do this in short blurbs. Record anything you may wish to know or consider about that issue at hand. Try to come up with at least ten aspects that you would like to know or understand about the matter before you attempt to come up with a solution.

On a separate piece of paper, start exploring where, how, and when you might find more information. Be sure to think about who might help you with possible answers or approaches to these problems.

Exercise—What is keeping you from greater achievement and success?

Getting to success simply comes down to a matter of problem solving. When you know where you want to go, you can work backward and list all the things keeping you from success. After you make your list, ask the questions related to each one of those items.

- How can I eliminate this obstacle?
- Can I go around it?
- Does this problem need a solution?
- What weaknesses do I have that are keeping me from this goal?
- Who can help?
- What strengths do I have that can compensate?
- Who could help me with these specific questions?
- What habit would I need to develop in order to get a better result?

When we spend time to ask productive questions, we come up with valuable answers to solve the challenges holding us back from the things we want most in life.

Ask appropriate questions—Questions to consider

- What will I need to become in order to prepare for the goals I want to achieve?
- What is it that is currently keeping me from greater achievement or success?
- What will have to happen to allow that event?
- How will I know when I have arrived?
- How will I continue that success beyond that event?
- What price am I willing to pay to get there?
- What will I have to sacrifice to get there?
- How can I deal with a specific obstacle?
- Who can help me with specific aspects of the task?

Act with Confidence

*It's not who you are that holds you back;
it's who you think you're not.*

When I was seven, I was invited to participate in a talent show at our church. My talent was to play piano. I was still very new at the piano and had just started learning how to play with both hands at the same time.

The song that was chosen for me was "Oh Suzanna." I practiced and practiced to get ready for this performance.

When I got to the church and saw how many people began to fill the seats, I began to be nervous. I began to secretly wish that maybe I had gotten even more practice in. My confidence was quickly fading. As each act on the program performed and we got closer to my name, I grew more and more nervous.

Suddenly it was my turn. I could feel my heart beating almost to the point of popping out of my chest. My hands were shaking, and although I was never going to hit more than three piano keys at a time, I couldn't even remember where to start.

My mother took me to the stairs on the stage and told me that I would do fine. "Just play like you practiced." How could she have confidence in me? Did she not see the vast audience expecting incredible things from me? I didn't get it.

As we stopped in the stairwell ready to enter the stage, several of the members in our church turned to me and also said, "You're going to do great." At first I wondered, "How can they believe in me?" They hadn't even heard me play before.

The curtain then went down on the last act, and the people on stage motioned for me to get ready to come out and take my place at the piano before the curtain lifted again. Although I was prepared and others were confident, I was still nervous. Then I had an epiphany: I decided that although I was nervous, I could act confident.

I strode out with the actions of a polished concert pianist. I placed my music book open before me and rested my hands above the keys, poised to begin. My heart was beating ferociously inside my chest. But I tried to look like I knew exactly what I was doing.

The curtains opened, and I began my rendition of "Oh Suzanna" three notes at a time. I maintained the appearance of confidence throughout. Even my fingers seemed to believe my act and cooperated, hitting mostly all correct notes.

When it all ended, the applause let me know that it had gone well. Still in the act of the confident concert pianist, I rose and took a majestic bow. My nervousness was now gone, and the experience gave me even more confidence for future recitals.

While I didn't know it then, I had just experienced the principle of acting with confidence. And that principle helped me to see a successful ending to one of the most frightening experiences of my life.

Fake it 'til you make it vs. acting with confidence

You've probably heard the saying that you can "fake it 'til you make it." I want to state unequivocally that faking it is not what I experienced at the piano concert. Faking it just won't cut it in creating lasting success.

Faking it implies that we have not put in the preparation. Faking it implies that we act falsely to portray something that is not us and that we have not qualified to be. You've probably heard of horror stories about salespeople who give promises and commitments in relation to products and services that just are not true. It always gets found out.

Acting with confidence is something different. We decide what we will become, and we genuinely start working toward that direction. We put in the practice, and because of our preparation, we are qualified to play the part.

You are only out integrity if you are not actually moving in that direction. When we are moving toward that destination, we can begin to act with confidence and with a spirit of success in that direction.

Not too long ago I had an interesting conversation with a friend of mine on this principle of acting with confidence. She is a neuroscientist and studies the workings of the human brain. She had some interesting insights into acting with confidence. She stated, "Acting with confidence or acting with depression trains the brain how to process experiences."

When we act a certain way and believe specific things about ourselves, our brain begins to form neural pathways that dictate how we process the information our brain receives. If we act with confidence, our brain instructs us to begin to see things with greater confidence, and we begin to see the outside world reflect our inner confidence.

When we act with depression or doubt, our mind constructs scenarios to support our inner thought patterns.

Psychologist William James stated that "motion effects emotion." If we move with confidence, we begin to feel the emotions of confidence. It is for this reason that when we act with genuine confidence, it becomes a true principle of self-creation.

Summary: We can create our destiny by acting the part of who we truly wish to become.

The effect on others

It has been said that animals can smell fear. Humans can too. It's crystal clear in business and life when someone shows up unprepared. It just comes off as awkward and disjointed. When we are confident and genuinely have a level of competence, others will quickly respond.

We must be cautious again that integrity and skill are attached to this confidence. If we are just boastful or prideful about our abilities without real substance, we will come off with very negative results.

In my business I am regularly at events surrounded by motivational speakers and trainers. It has been exciting for me to meet so many powerful people. Two of the components that I have found that make the really great ones exceptionally great are that they know how to deliver both passion and power.

What I mean by passion is the ability to get passionate about what they share and how they deliver their message. This is the ultimate in acting confident. They have a unique ability through their excitement to get other people excited about their vision of what they are teaching. People leave their seminars at an all-time emotional high.

Power is the other essential element the excellent speaker has. The top speakers know how to deliver a message with passion and acting in confidence, but they also know how to deliver the goods. They ensure that when their participants leave their seminars and the passion wears off, they still have powerful tools that can create better results and more-successful strategies in their lives.

If you just have passion and get an audience excited with no substance, you are faking it. If you can deliver a powerful message with passion, you are the real deal. As you act with confidence, you will be creating your future deliberately. Self-creation magnifies our ability to accomplish great things.

We teach people how to treat us.

Two men enter into a boardroom. One is dressed in a crisp suit, sharp tie. He carries in his hand a leather briefcase with gold knobs. His hair is combed neatly, and he is clean-shaven.

The other man enters the room wearing blue jeans with a rip in one knee. His T-shirt advertises a brand-new heavy-metal rock band. He carries a skateboard with a neon skeleton on the bottom. His hair is dyed with purple tips, and he hasn't used a razor for a few days.

They both sit at the table and offer you an investment opportunity. The man with the suit pulls out neatly organized folders. The other fellow puts out a soiled napkin with a few notes after searching through each of his pockets. And slides it across the table to you. What are your first impressions?

While both may have an interesting opportunity, how they appear and act will have a significant impact on your decision. How we dress, act, and present ourselves will have a direct effect on how people respond to us.

Actions can change feelings.

Earlier in this volume we talked about how feelings precede actions. What we think about most will determine how we feel about certain things and ultimately how we will act. The same is true in reverse. How we act can have a profound effect on how we feel and think.

A friend of mine conducts seminars for couples. Not too long ago, she shared with me an interesting story of a couple on the verge of divorce.

They had started out happy, full of love and optimism about the future. But arguing and contention had crept slowly into their relationship. It had all but choked the remaining positive feelings away. They were sarcastic and bitter toward each other. Plans were in the making for separation and possible divorce.

Along the way a lot of different strategies and counsel had been given, and slowly the situation was changed and love was restored. The couple later reported back the single most important advice that they were given. The advice that made the most difference to their situation was to simply start acting lovingly toward each other. What they did eventually changed what they felt. As they acted, so they became.

Exercise—Who will you be in five years?

Imagine in your mind what your life will look like in five years.

- What will your lifestyle be like?
- What will your relationships be?
- If you had all the answers that you needed to create success, would that change your daily interactions with people?

Think carefully about what you would really be like. Make sure this image is genuinely in harmony with who and what you wish to become.

The challenge: Why can't you be that person right now? I challenge you to start behaving as though you were already there. By doing so, you will take a greater leap toward creating the ideal future for yourself and creating the person you want to be.

Exercise—Who's in your corner?

Sometimes in frightening situations it can be difficult to act with confidence. However, we have all had moments when we have been able to face frightening situations because our peers or family members have been with us. The goal of this exercise is to remind you of the strength of those who believe in you.

We all have many supporters and friends who believe in us. They can't be with us in all the situations we encounter. But they can be with us in our thoughts.

Sometimes it can help to think about how you will share a particular experience in the future with your supporters. Before going into a frightening situation, think about sharing it later and specifically *whom* you will share it with. When you do this and visualize yourself sharing the experience in a positive way, the fearful feelings associated with the experience dissipate.

Confidence then comes and you can face the experience with bold courage. Confidence is gained by facing frightening experiences with courage. Sometimes the only way to do that is simply to jump right in.

It's like when you are at the swimming pool. It is oftentimes far easier to jump right in than it is to stand at the side and think about it while testing the water temperature with your big toe. The more we stand on the side and think about it, the harder it becomes to overcome the fear.

Each time we jump in, we gain more confidence that things will be fine the next time we approach a swimming pool.

Act with confidence—Questions to consider

- What am I afraid of that keeps me from being confident?
- What would a person with the success I am seeking act like?
- When are the hardest moments for me to act with confidence?
- How can I remind myself to act with more confidence?
- How can I face fearful situations with greater confidence?
- Who will I be five years from now if I continue to do what I am doing now?
- What are my current behaviors costing me?
- Who do I want to be five years from now?

Average vs. Extraordinary

Don't lower your expectations to meet your performance.
Raise your level of performance to meet your expectations.
Expect the best of yourself,
and then do what is necessary to make it a reality.
——Ralph Marston

Average is defined as *being typical*. Typical is not something that stands out. Nor is it something that produces extraordinary results. High achievers are never typical, average, or normal. They are extraordinary. That should be your goal!

While there are many people who are satisfied to be average, my assumption is that the reason you selected this book was because you would prefer to be extraordinary.

What is your standard of excellence? What is extraordinary to you? Oftentimes we let the idea of extraordinary frighten us. At first glance it may seem that it will take too much work and require a high level of commitment.

Extraordinary is found in doing little things in an extraordinary way. Johann Wolfgang Goethe said it this way: "To have more you must become more."

Hard work

Michelangelo made an interesting observation once. He said, "If people knew how hard I had to work to gain my mastery, it wouldn't seem wonderful at all."

To be extraordinary, you need to put in hard work in developing the little things. I found this firsthand when I was working a summer job in college. My job was to sell pest control door-to-door in southern California. The days were hot, and it was easy to justify taking a break to sit in the shade or go find a place to get some lemonade. But I found that when the others stopped, if I kept going for one more street of contacts that my paycheck would be significantly larger. Just one more street was my commitment.

Each day of one or two extra streets added up, and soon I found that my level of success was dramatically different from that of those who were satisfied to stop at what was simply required.

The same is true on many levels. If you would experience lasting success, you must learn the principle of over-delivering or going the extra mile. When you over-deliver, people will seek you out as the one who is genuinely concerned about them and their business. They will seek you out, and you will be considered the expert and person to trust.

Finding your uniqueness

What makes you extraordinary while everyone else in the room is average? Think about it. Everyone feels that he or she is unique and special—and they are right. We each have unique things that make us very different from everyone else. But if you were to ask one hundred people what makes them different—and I have—you would find that more than 80 percent of the people would give you similar answers. The differences most people value aren't that different at all.

Everyone is unique, with special gifts and attributes. Very few people have invested the time and consideration to find out what it is that really makes them unique and extraordinary. And the most unique people are the ones who actually do something with their discovery.

Doug Hall, author of the book *Jump Start Your Business Brain*, lists one of the three key things that aids in business success is to have a business that is *dramatically different*. The trouble is that too often we deliver our business in the same way that everyone else does and expects. In the end, we get the same results that everyone else is getting.

Caution: It is important to point out that being different does not necessarily mean a person is extraordinary. We have all met many people who are *very* different. (Just take a walk in Times Square in New York City, and you'll understand what I mean.) Often these "different" people are not really leading lives that I would call extraordinary.

In addition to being dramatically different, we need to be dynamically different. To be dynamic is to be active, energetic, forceful, and powerful. In what way are your differences dynamic? In what ways are they contributing to greater success and achievement?

Dynamic differences are not accidents.

Dynamic differences don't come about by accident. They come through exploration and consideration. They will come as you use your imagination to look for ways to make a difference that is active, energetic, forceful, powerful, and most of all valuable.

Albert Einstein said, "Imagination is more important than knowledge."

What can you imagine and create that will make you different?

What will you do that will cause you to be remembered as extraordinary? How can you deliver that difference in a dynamic way?

Your most important asset is your ability to imagine and create. Are you using that gift enough in your daily activities? These are important questions.

Many business owners come up with something so different that they lose their audience. They make their offering so bizarre that the customer just doesn't understand. You need to be careful that you select something that will strengthen your message, not weaken it. Your difference should make sense to your customer and be valuable.

The best way to beat your competition is to have a better idea. Once you have a few ideas, it will be valuable to take those thoughts to a peer group and get their input before sharing it with the world. Sometimes we get too close to an idea and can't always see if it works. You will soon discover which ideas hold the most value for your company. Don't forget to consider the following questions:

- Which ideas can you easily adopt and implement?
- Which ideas do others find valuable too?

If you do the same things that ordinary people are doing, you will get the same ordinary results. It's as simple as that. Ordinary people create ordinary lives. They solve problems in an ordinary way. They do their work in an ordinary way. They get ordinary results. If you want something more, you have to do something more.

Average vs. extraordinary—Questions to consider

- What is the difference between average and extraordinary?
- What do I choose to be?
- What am I currently doing in an average way?
- How can I do things in a more extraordinary way than I do now?
- How can I go the extra mile?
- How am I different from my competitors?
- In what ways can I be dynamically different?
- How can I add more creativity or imagination to my efforts?

Excerpts from the Success Interviews: Richard Kiel

Richard is a Hollywood actor best known for his roles as the villain Jaws in the James Bond series. Richard has also appeared in such films and TV projects as *Happy Gilmore* with Adam Sandler, *Inspector Gadget 2*, *Cannonball Run 2*, *The Longest Yard*, *Twilight Zone* (the original TV series), *Gilligan's Island*, *I Dream of Jeannie*, and countless other films. Recently Richard was the voice of several characters in the new Disney animated show *Tangled*. And by the way, did I mention that Richard is over seven feet tall?

Doug: Hi, Richard. It's great to chat as usual. But this time a little more formally for this interview. Let's see if we can give our readers a little background on you that they may not know. While you've achieved a lot in your career, it didn't come easy. Tell us a little bit about that journey.

Richard: It took a lot of perseverance and investing back in myself and my career. I probably ran fifteen or twenty full-page trade ads in the *Hollywood Reporter* and *Variety* along the way. When I did something worthwhile, I would bring it to the attention of the industry. You know, the casting people, producers, and writers. And that really worked. People got to know me, and they would see an ad and get to know a little bit about what I was doing.

Doug: So how did you really get started in the movie business? Let's go back to when you were a kid. I don't think a lot of people know about how you really got started.

Richard: Well, my dad died; he was only fifty-three years old. And our appliance and TV store had been suffering because of the recession of 1958. That was the year that he died. And then they were putting in a large freeway nearby our store and they put a big pile of dirt in front of half of the street in front of us. So there was no parking. You had to walk a block and a half to get to our store.

Doug: That must have been tough for people wanting to buy furniture.

Richard: I think it was really a part of my dad having a heart attack, because there was really nothing he could do about it. But anyway, we were able to stay open for about a year after that—my mom and I. But we just never seemed to be able to catch up. You know, with the problems that caused. And both my mom and I had to go out and get other jobs. So we closed up the family business. And my mom got a job at a cemetery, and she was able to do really well. But she had house payments and car payments. She had to, because my dad didn't really leave a lot in insurance. But she was able to use her bad experiences to share with other people in the funeral business to help them prepare to avoid what she had gone through. So I started with them too after a while. And they had a script and I followed it, and I did pretty well.

It was one of those things where you build up payments, like insurance that would come in every month. I kind of got burned out with the cemetery thing; I was too young to be dealing with that. I mean, my dad had just died.

So from our store I had experience with appliance repair and I went to repairing appliances. It was really tough to get a job.

I had an aunt who was a movie and television fan, and she said, "Why don't you get into the movies? Somebody with your height and size could really do something." And she kind of gave me some ideas. I thought to myself, *that makes sense.*

Doug: So your aunt is really the one who got you thinking about movies?

Richard: Yeah, she thought I could dress up like the Jolly Green Giant or something. She kind of gave me some ideas. Size was always something that I needed to think about. To buy a sports coat back then was tough. They didn't have any of these Big & Tall stores. I think there was one in downtown Los Angeles. But I wasn't really aware of them at that time. In order to have a sports coat, I had to have it custom-made. Even back then, it took about five weeks of the average salary to buy a sports coat. And I couldn't fit in a Volkswagen or Camaro, so I had to have a bigger car.

Doug: So you've probably never gone shopping for a Smart car?

Richard: My parents bought me a queen-size bed, which was six foot eight, and I'm seven foot two.

Doug: I think a Smart car could fit on top of a queen-size bed.

Richard: Probably. Everything is expensive when you are bigger. The king-size beds were about six or seven weeks' wages. So everything for someone big is expensive. I used to joke and say I bought the biggest shoes I could find and I wear the boxes they came in. The only shoes I could get as a teenager were postman shoes. And again, they were kind of pricey. So I thought maybe becoming an actor would be something I could do and it also would pay more. I could utilize my size to be able to pay for what it costs to be so big. So I decided to do that.

I was at the local gas station one day, and there was a guy there working on a Pepsi machine. And he seemed like a nice guy, and I asked him if there were any jobs available. And he drove me to the Pepsi Company, and I found out that they didn't really have any jobs available at the time. This guy really wanted to help me, so he told me about a guy he knew that had a nightclub. There are a lot of Hollywood types that go there. He said Elvis Presley used to sometimes go there. "Maybe you could get a job there and get discovered and be in the movies." So he took me out there and introduced me to the people.

It just happened that the doorman bouncer was a guy named Red West. One of Elvis Presley's cronies. And Red had used some martial arts on a customer that got out of line, and the insurance company for this club wanted to get rid of him. And I just happened to be there at the right time and they hired me.

Doug: How old were you at that time?

Richard: I was about twenty. And I wasn't even old enough to drink, but here I was checking IDs. The vice cops were in there all the time. But they didn't bother me. I guess they just couldn't believe somebody that big couldn't be twenty-one. Elvis did come in one time, and I did meet him. And other celebrities and other Hollywood people came in also. But I couldn't have been trying to get into movies at a worse time. There was a strike going on. An actors' strike or a writers' strike or something. I can't remember. And everything was pretty much shut down. But I let people know—I think that's important. I let people know that I was trying to get into the movies and that I was an actor. One of the guys that came in there was a horse wrangler named Pinto Spahn. His dad owned the famous Spahn ranch.

Doug: The same ranch where the Manson family hung out?

Richard: Yeah. Pinto was a cowboy-type guy, and he was impressed with me. And I got a list of the agents. About fifty, maybe eighty, agents and their addresses. And I started going from one to the other. But the ones that I got in to see always asked the same questions. What had I done? And I hadn't done anything. Did I have a Screen Actors Guild card? No. They were just very … anyway, what could you do? "I'm sorry; we're just not taking any new clients."

I got down to one on the list: Herman Zimmerman. And he seemed like a pretty nice guy. He wasn't so negative. He said to me, "Well, Richard, if you still want to be an actor in six months, come back and see me." In the meantime, the strike ended. But nobody seemed to want to represent me. So I saw a job in the newspaper for a guy with some technical experience and sales experience for Hammond organs. I was perfect for it. So I started for them.

But one day I got a phone call. And I pick up the phone, and this guy comes on the phone and says, "I'm Bob Gilbert, and Pinto Spahn told me about you. Is it true that you're over seven feet tall?" I said yeah. And he said, "You weigh over three hundred pounds?" I said yeah. And he said, "Well, how would you like to be in a television pilot?" And I said, "What does it pay?" At that time, this is like 1960, and a typical job delivering water paid sixty to seventy dollars a week. And he said this was a hundred dollars a day. "Can you come down and see me today?" I went down there, and it didn't start paying a hundred dollars a day. They wanted to start out by doing a test. They were testing three leading men for the role of the Phantom, based on the comic book. You know, the guy with the purple suit.

Doug: And the skull ring.

Richard: Yeah, that's right. So they said, "We won't pay you for this test. But there is a good chance that it will work for you and you'll get in the pilot. In addition, we will give you the film from the test so you will have some film on yourself." So I thought, *what the heck? Why not?* But then the guy took it one step further and said, "There is one of the actors that we really want to look good. He's a really nice guy." I found out later his parents put money in the pilot.

Doug: Well, that helps.

Richard: Ha-ha, gives him a leg up. This guy was a stuntman that had been doubling Bob Hope. And they wanted me to go out and work with him. So that he would look really good. And they thought it would help me too, so I would look even better. So I agreed to that and went out there, and he taught me how to throw punches without hitting anybody and how to sell it. And how to make it really look good and how to react.

So on my way back, I stopped to chat with one of the people I'd told about my dream to be in movies who I'd met at the nightclub. His name was Bob Coultier. It was close to closing time and the door was open. So I walked in. And he wasn't in his office. But I heard some voices upstairs. So I walked upstairs to tell him about this little success I was having. And I walked in and the door was open, and there were three guys in there. They had been drinking. And Bob was intoxicated and tried to introduce me to the others present. So I shook hands. And it turns out that one of the men was a film executive. And he told me to come by and see him. So I went up to his office a day or so later, and he had half a dozen people working there. And when I got to his office, he said, "Come on in," and he was on the phone.

He motioned for me to sit down. And he said, "Bill, I got the guy right in my office as we speak … How tall is he?" He looked at me, and I indicated with my fingers, seven and then two. He says, "He's almost eight feet tall." And then he asks, "How much does he weigh?" And then he looked at me again, and I did three and ten with my fingers. And he says to the guy on the phone, "He weighs almost four hundred pounds … Yeah, I'll send him right over." So this was the first time I saw this guy sober and he's giving me a job. So he says, "You're going to go see a guy named William Conrad, and he is the producer of a show called *Klondike*, starring James Coburn." And in the meantime, I also got the pilot for the Phantom. So I went back to see the agent I spoke about earlier, Herman Zimmerman. He was the least pessimistic. I said, "Mr. Zimmerman, I managed to get two lead roles on my own, and I now have a SAG card. Do you want to be my agent or not?" And he said yes.

So I was with him for about twenty-five years, until he died. That's one of the reasons I wrote my book *Making It Big in the Movies*—to let people know that it wasn't easy. It took a lot of optimism and hard work to go out and see all those agents and to agree to do the test for free and go out and do all the extra work to look good. Normally when people ask me how I got started, they don't want to hear that it was a lot of work.

Doug: I loved your book. And that is an important message that you share: persistence and sticking to it. Hard work and commitment

were all so essential to your being successful in your career. It was so interesting for me to see that the harder you tried, the more impressive the doors were that opened for you. I think there are many lessons in that for people wanting to create their own successes.

Richard: That's one thing a lot of new actors forget: that it is a business. It needs to be approached like a business. I worked at it. I worked the plan and was optimistic, not pessimistic. And I didn't let other people's pessimism stop me. My feeling was that there were shows with fairly big heroes, and they weren't going to look good beating up people that were smaller than them. I felt that there was a need and I should be able to fill that need. Some people don't see how they can fill a need.

Doug: I think that is common: people try to service an industry doing what everyone else is doing, and they don't get results. It's easy to get discouraged quickly, and they give up.

Richard: That's true. And most of the people when they saw me, they would think in terms of Frankenstein or monster-type stuff or Lenny from *Of Mice and Men*. So either you played a monster or you played a dummy. I was fortunate that the first couple of jobs I had, I didn't play a total dummy. I tried to find a way to break away from those stereotypes but create memorable roles. It wasn't just about my size; it was about creating a more memorable character. That's what made characters like Jaws work so well. And it all came about from taking a risk and seeing yourself doing that. And trying to do something about it.

Along the way, one of my first movies was *Eegah*. I learned a lot from the producer. I went on a promotional tour with his son. Not glamorous. The first stop, for example, was a McDonalds. But I realized from him that it is important to tell your story. This guy would march us into radio stations and TV stations, and they would do stories on us. That's when I realized that there was a need to fill. They need to have stories, and if you present yourself, you get the stories.

Doug: Your career really demonstrates how you can make a unique appearance become an advantage for you rather than a hindrance.

Richard: And as I became a success, it was still difficult. While I was doing the movies, I was still selling cars. I was doing good as a salesman. I won a color TV and a trip to Hawaii and a fancy watch. I was a go-getter and people liked me. And if they didn't buy a new car from me, they would come back with their friends. Then I got this movie *The Longest Yard*. You remember the convicts playing football against the guards in the prison? But at first I couldn't get an interview. The casting director was from New York City, and she was told by the director that he only wanted professional football players. But I thought this would be a great role for me. I felt like I belonged in that movie. My agent was affiliated with two other guys. He merged with Stevens Grey and associates. And I mentioned it to these guys, and they were casting for the producer of *The Longest Yard* on another movie. The guy's name was Al Ruddy; he was one of the producers of the original *Godfather* movie. He had the largest office at Paramount. And he said, "I can get you in to meet Al Ruddy. Why don't we start there?"

So I meet Al Ruddy. And he said, "I think you'd be a great character for this movie. I am going to set up an interview with Robert Aldridge." So he did. Aldridge did his best to discourage me. He did the *Dirty Dozen* and had a bad experience with a few actors who were wimpy. So he said, "Tell me about your football experience." And so I told him that I had played football in high school, but then got busy in the movie business. I told him I still played a little football with Brodie and the boys every now and then. He said, "Brodie and the boys? Are you talking about John Brodie? Quarterback for the San Francisco 49ers?" "Yeah, John Brodie." I had already arranged this because I knew he was going to ask me about football.

Doug: You mean John Brodie who was the NFL most valuable player in 1970?

Richard: Yeah.

Doug: That would get his attention.

Richard: I'd actually arranged this through a friend of mine who knew John Brodie, to be able to play ball with him—if I had to. So Aldridge said, "I'd like to see that." So I said, "The next time we play, I can give you a call and let you know about it." So he said to call his secretary and let her know, and he'd come out and see that. I think he thought it was a line of BS. But he said, "Richard, let me tell you something. Where this movie is going to be shot ... We're going to be in a little town in Georgia. We are going to be scrimmaging for weeks on end. Do you think you can handle the pain?" I took a real gamble, and I kicked into my best acting gear and I looked right at him and I said, "Is it okay if I hurt them too?" I got into what I thought might be an interesting character, and he said, "No, no, we don't want anyone getting hurt. It's just a movie." So then he kind of softened up toward me and reminded me to give him a call when I was going to be working out with Brodie. I arranged it. And soon after, I got a call to come in and do a reading. And to make a long story short, I got the job.

Doug: That really demonstrates how important it is to be committed and not take no for an answer.

Richard: You got it. And that wasn't the only time that hard work and determination paid off. On another occasion I could not get an interview for a new movie of the week called *The Barbary Coast*. The role was for a nightclub bouncer named Moose Moran. But I couldn't get an interview. So I wrote a letter to the producer and director, saying that I was like the character and even had nightclub experience. I outlined all of my film experience, including *The Longest Yard*, which had done well, and sent the letters to them certified. I informed them that I had not been able to get an interview and felt that we should have the opportunity to meet. Soon after, my agent called and said that they had gotten my letter and wanted to meet me. To make a long story short, I got the role. Now the reason why I am telling you this story is that this movie became a weekly series. But it only ran for thirteen weeks. But the BBC in England was famous for buying up shows that only had a short run because they could get them real cheap. The continuity lady for the James Bond people saw it and suggested to Cubby Broccoli that he interview me when he was in Los Angeles. I was working on the *Silver Streak* and got a phone call from my agent, and he said that Cubby Broccoli wanted to interview me. At first I didn't know who he was. And he said, "He's the producer of the James Bond movies."

Doug: You knew who James Bond was?

Richard: Oh yeah. And so he wanted to interview me tomorrow at lunch at the Beverly Hills Hotel. So I needed to take a longer lunch. So I asked the first assistant on the *Silver Streak* about getting a longer lunch. And he said, "Cubby Broccoli? Of course." And that's how it all came about. So if it hadn't been for *The Longest Yard* and *The Barbary Coast,* and going after my goal and not giving up, and not taking no for an answer and finding a way to do it, it never would have happened for the James Bond movies.

Doug: There are so many important lessons from your experiences: determination, being prepared, not taking no for an answer, looking for solutions.

Richard: When you talk about preparation, I would go to the acting coaches and take some of the money that I was going to be making and prepare for those challenging roles. And get help and prepare the best I possibly could.

Doug: What does success mean to you today?

Richard: Well, to me it's happiness, family, security, being fulfilled in life, helping others. Spreading happiness is important. Those are the things that I find success is. And of course, being able to pay the bills along the way.

3—What Do You Really Want?

If you want to live a happy life, tie it to a goal, not to people or things.
—Albert Einstein

Most people have no idea what it is that they really want out of life. They allow things to happen to them, and they react to circumstances, rather than create opportunities. If by chance they recognize opportunities that happen to show up in a relatively convenient way, perhaps they do something about them.

Successful people understand that they control many circumstances in their lives and they have power to create the opportunities they want by design, rather than default.

We do have control over what happens in our lives. We can make choices that affect the way our situations will be tomorrow. Without knowing what you want, you can't really decide where you are going.

How will your future look?

How will your future look? When was the last time you asked that question? If you are like most people, you may have occasionally thought about it, but you really haven't invested significant consideration to decide where you are really headed.

When you walk into a travel agency, you have in mind a destination. Perhaps you may have spoken to others who have previously been to this location or even seen it on TV. The agent can show you brochures and talk about what you might visit while in that area. You plan the trip and you follow the plan. You eventually enjoy the destination and come home with pictures and souvenirs of the visit. You can do the same with your own future. In fact, why not have a little fun and sit down and make a travel brochure describing the future you would like to create?

Now ask the important question: "Are you actually heading there?" Have you purchased the tickets, so to speak, through the choices you are making today? If something needs to be created differently today to reach a different destination tomorrow, are you prepared to do the work? That is really the only way your future can change. You have to do something to change it. Your desired future will not arrive by accident.

Have real expectations.

Most people have a hard time really figuring out what their future will look like. They often say, "It'll be nice when I retire. I will then be able to do anything I want and no one will bother me." They dream that every day in the future will be sunny and relaxing. The truth is that this might be the case at times, but for the most part, there will still be everyday life. There will be rainy days, setbacks, challenges, and problems to resolve. What will the future really look like?

Frustration comes because people do not have expectations that are realistic. When you are realistic, you will find that your journey to success will become more enjoyable.

Get real expectations!

- What will your financial situation look like if you pursue the course you are currently on?
- What will your relationships situation be like?
- What will your hobby time look like?
- What will be your obligations to other people?
- What other obligations will you have in the future?
- What work will you be responsible for?

> Desire is the starting point of all achievement, not a hope, not a wish, but a keen pulsating desire which transcends everything.
> —Napoleon Hill

Seeing that future life for what it really may be like will help you create the life that you really want. It will also help you to see that indeed there will be responsibilities there too. Knowing that life will not be easier (especially if you do nothing in the present) can also be a powerful motivator to get busy creating the life you really want.

It is common when asking people about their future to discover they see a heavenly bliss without responsibilities. It is my opinion that even when we die, if we get to heaven there will still be things to do. It won't be a swamp or a stagnant piece of land. It will be active and productive. If you consider the kinds of people who would get there, could it be any other way?

Priorities

Often we may say we know what we want but we are unable to get it. As I have observed the most successful people on the planet, and many who were less successful, an interesting pattern emerged. Successful people know what they want. They know how to quickly zero in on the most important tasks and get them done. They quickly recognize the least-effective tasks and leave them undone.

Unsuccessful people for the most part inject extensive effort to work hard on tasks that do not provide significant benefit or any return toward the overall goal. Active effort alone does not create success. Success must be centered in effective activities. This ability to recognize priorities comes from understanding what you want and the direction you are going.

Exercise—Priorities count.

Make a list of the activities that you engage in each day. Divide the day into ten- to fifteen-minute increments. Now beside each of these activities, put a yes if it actually fits with your major goals and a no if it does not. Experience has shown that most people will immediately recognize that a majority of their activities are not contributing to their most important goals.

After you have found the activities that are relevant to your goals, number them to discover which ones are most effective at creating the desired results. Similar activities should be priorities every day from now on. Have these activities been treated like priorities in the past? If not, what can you do to change that? Consider what activities should be added to this priority list and where they should be placed in terms of priority in your daily schedule.

ROE

A great consideration when prioritizing these activities is to consider their ROE (return on effort) in relationship to your major goals. Notice that this is different from ROI (return on investment), which is often a consideration when investing money.

ROE is different in that it measures all efforts. If something requires high effort, even though it is inexpensive, the effort is still less productive. Look for activities that pay high dividends toward getting to your goals. Money, time, effort, and resources are all valuable commodities that should not be squandered.

What do you really want?—Questions to consider

- What does my future look like?
- What actions will lead me to the future that I want most?
- What current actions and habits are leading me away from the future I want most?
- What obstacles do I see in my future that I can prevent today?
- What are my most important priorities?
- Why?
- What is the priority right now?
- What activities are providing me the greatest ROE?
- How are my activities progressing me toward my greatest goals?

Get Clarity

Clarity of mind means clarity of passion, this is why a great and clear mind loves ardently and sees distinctly what he loves.
—Blaise Pascal

Clarity is one of the great mysteries of achievement. Many people have a hard time describing what they really want because they have never taken the time to consider carefully what it might be.

Define the outcome.

"Can I take your order please?" If you've ever been through a drive-through, you've heard that question. Your answer to that question will ultimately determine what you will see a few windows farther down the line.

What do you think your outcome would be if you just kept driving without describing what you want? Of course, it would be a surprise, and you might not like it.

Many people are currently placing an order in their lives the same way. They don't know what they want, and when they get to that next window, they get whatever happens to be there. Successful people don't approach their lives that way. The choices they make are deliberate and concise orders of exactly what they want.

They take the time to plan it out. They explore the details of what the future looks like, and they know when they have arrived. They recognize that life is like taking a trip and using a map. The more specific you are able to become, the more likely you will arrive quickly and on schedule.

A goal that is specific and clear becomes attainable and near.

Million-dollar briefcase

My friend Brian Tracy uses a really great analogy. He says, "If I told you there was a briefcase with a million dollars in it sitting on a back porch in the city somewhere, how long do you think it would take you to get it? If you didn't know where it was, you could literally search for a lifetime. But what if I told you the street—would that help? Or what if I told you the address? Would that speed things up?"

Of course it would. The same is true of the accomplishments you are trying to create in your life. The more specific you can be, the more likely it will be that you will find that million-dollar briefcase.

What if I don't have my exact destination?

Changing and redefining your direction is something that happens all the time. And there is no harm in it. In fact, it is better to run in the general direction you want to go than to do nothing at all.

Think of this question: Is it easier to change the direction a train is going when it is moving or standing still? A heavy object like a train is easier to redirect when it is moving. The momentum that you have created to get started may very well be employed to get to a new destination that you have discovered to be more inviting and appealing while on the route.

It is also possible that from where you stand today you may not see your final destination. Perhaps all you can identify is the direction. When I was in high school, no one ever told me I could be an author or a motivational speaker. It just wasn't an option to consider. But as I pursued a course toward business and a love of teaching, my real destination presented itself.

Life is really a matter of gathering options and considering opportunities. The more we gather, the more avenues open up for us to explore.

The question "Why?" is a key.

To illustrate what I mean, let me share the following experience. Prior to an event I spoke at in Scottsdale, Arizona, I had lunch with a gentleman who told me his goal was to be a millionaire by the conclusion of the year. He asked me for tips on how he could get there quickly. My first question caught him off guard; I asked *why* he wanted to be a millionaire. He shrugged and said that he just wanted to have that kind of money in the bank. Again I asked him *why* that was important to him. Again he shrugged and said he wasn't really sure what I meant; wasn't the idea of having a million dollars enough?

I didn't believe it was. I didn't believe that was a powerful enough motivating force. We continued to talk about the reasons why he had selected that goal. Soon we discovered that it wasn't really the money he wanted at all. It was the experiences that the financial situation could provide. He began to list the things that a million-dollar lifestyle would make available for him. He talked about the experiences, the relationships, the opportunities, and a host of other reasons. As he listed these reasons, he began to form an emotional attachment to a new end goal that had to do with the experiences. He now had real clarity about his goal and the real reason why.

Understanding *why* gives you a greater clarity, emotional connection to the end result, and much more motivating power.

Answering the question "Why?" tells you if you are on the right path. ~~~~~~~~~~~~~~~~~~

It has been said that people are often so busy climbing the ladder to success that they are devastated when they reach the top only to find that it has been leaning against the wrong wall. By asking why, you may be able to determine that some of your needs might be better met by following a different route than the one you initially chose.

Exercise—Vision boards with a special ingredient ~~~~~~~~~~~~~~~~~~~~~~~~~~~~~~~~~~

At home or in the office, some people have vision boards with pictures clipped from magazines and catalogs.

Let me help you power-charge your vision board. Add to your board descriptions and emotionally charged words that provide the reasons why the items depicted there are important to you. Be sure to get clear on what these things really mean to you and why you want them in your life.

And as far as images go, I would encourage you to try to include images that stir you emotionally—images that really answer not only what, but why.

Clarity gives direction. ~~~~~~

Gaining direction is an essential part of making your action effective. When we have clarity, we can be confident that we will have more power to recognize the direction of the steps we need to take to get there.

Exercise—Get Clarity. ~~~~~~

Select one of the key goals you are currently working on in your goal journal and write all of the reasons why this goal is important to you. Keep probing deeper and deeper into the reasons why until you can go no further. Probing in this way will serve two purposes:

1) It will allow you to see what wants and needs are really being met through this goal. As you do this, you may discover that perhaps there may be an easier way to satisfy this need than committing

to the initial goal you thought about. You may discover a different goal altogether.

2) When you can truly see why this goal is important to you, you will find great motivation and strength to keep working toward this goal.

Exercise—Which goal should I choose?

Sometimes I encounter people who feel that they have too many goals they want to accomplish and too many things that they want to do. They scratch their heads and say, "Well, I can't do them all. I'll lose my focus. But they are all interesting to me."

They are right that it is hard to do them all. It is easy to lose focus. In the end you may fall short of everything because your energy and effort simply run out. What can you do?

Here is an interesting exercise in clarity that has helped me to solve this problem.

After you have a list of major accomplishments that you are considering including in your life, write each one at the top of a separate paper. Then underneath write all the reasons why you want to have that experience in your life.

As you begin to see the quantity of reasons and the quality of reasons associated with each goal, you will see an order appear as to which goals are most important to you right now. You will then be able to attack the ones that are most meaningful to you first and have an idea of the goals to approach next.

Get clarity—Questions to consider

- What is it I want?
- Why do I want it?
- How will I know that I have arrived?
- Now that I am here, what will I do next?
- Why do I want to accomplish this goal?
- What will it bring into my life?
- How can I get emotionally connected to it?
- What experiences will it make available for me?
- How attached am I at an emotional level?

The Moment of Decision

The possibilities are numerous once we decide to act and not react.
—George Bernard Shaw

As I met with each of the four hundred top achievers I interviewed for my research into success, I asked a series of thought-provoking questions. One of the questions I asked was, "What was your greatest moment on your journey to success?"

Kelly Hrudy started as a young boy in Edmonton with dreams of playing hockey. But in the beginning, he wasn't very skilled. Most of the time when the neighborhood kids picked teams, he was left out until last. No one likes being left out and picked last.

One day Kelly decided that he didn't want to be left out anymore. He didn't want to be last. He wanted to be first.

From that moment forward, he dedicated himself to doing whatever it took to develop his skills. He committed extra hours of practice while others were watching TV. He kept fighting to succeed when things didn't come easily. When it was time to play, he gave everything he had until there was nothing left to give.

He began to turn the key to unlock the best he could be.

Eventually the boy that no one wanted on their team became a top NHL goalie, playing for teams like the Los Angeles Kings, New York Islanders, and San Jose Sharks.

He became such an expert at the sport that when it came time to retire, he was offered a job as a commentator on one of the most watched sports programs in the entire world, *Hockey Night in Canada*. But what was Kelly's greatest moment? Was it when he finally made the team? Keep reading to find out.

Anthony Daniels is best known for his portrayal of the world-famous protocol droid, C3PO, in the *Star Wars* films. Initially his parents tried to direct him to law school to be a lawyer. But along the way, he stumbled across an amateur dramatic society and found that his passion really was acting. Against the wishes of his parents, Anthony began to dedicate his energies to a career in the arts. He began to attract the attention of the BBC and then the

National Theatre. Shortly thereafter he met movie director George Lucas. As he began his first day of work on the *Star Wars* set, Anthony had no idea that he was about to create a role that would become a cultural icon for a generation of moviegoers. What was Anthony's greatest moment? Keep reading to find out.

Is the greatest moment the victory?

The greatest moment may be considered by many to be the final victory. To some, it's reaching superstar status or when your bank account bulges to overflowing. While those moments may be exciting, they are not your greatest moment.

The research I conducted determined that in order for a particular moment to be considered the greatest, it needed to answer three significant considerations.

- Which moment would have the most immediate consequences?
- Which moment would have the longest-lasting effect on the future?
- Which moment would have the most impact on you and those around you?

If we consider the criteria for the greatest moment, then it could be none other than the moment of decision.

Decision is the greatest moment.

Once Kelly and Anthony made a decision, everything changed for them forever. Decision changes everything.

When Kelly decided he was going to be great at hockey, his decision to be great changed everything. It changed his method of practice, changed his level of thinking, and totally changed his level of commitment.

When Anthony decided that acting was what he wanted to do instead of being a lawyer, his entire world changed. No longer was he investing his time trying to find where he belonged to please his parents. His focus changed from attending schools for things that didn't matter to him. He now dedicated his energy to developing his craft and taking advantage of opportunities that eventually put him in front of people like George Lucas.

Decision creates power.

When we eliminate the words and thoughts of *should, could,* and *would like to* and replace them with the total commitment that comes with making a decision, things change. Once we make a decision, power enters into our lives.

No longer are we teetering between uncertainty and progress. We are involved and committed.

Excuses

Decision eliminates excuses. When we truly decide to do something, excuses cease to exist. Excuses are a one-way ticket to failure. When we use excuses, we rationalize verbally why something cannot or has not been done. We never use excuses to convince others unless we have been convinced already that something is not possible. Excuse and belief cannot coexist at the same time. One will always destroy the other.

Successful people do not make excuses; they create solutions. People make excuses typically because they are afraid or too lazy to find or create solutions.

Decide for your future.

People avoid making a decision because they are afraid. They think their current situation won't allow them to make a change. This is silly. Think about it. Decisions have nothing to do with your current situation. You are already there and nothing is going to change that. A decision is a moment that affects your future. The decisions you make now are what is creating your future.

If you start making your decisions based on where you want to go, rather than where you currently are, you will start to see your life take a different direction. It will take the direction you want it to go, rather than continue in the direction it has been going.

Exercise—Make some decisions.

All of us have things that we want to do or have been thinking about doing for some time. Many of these things we have attached to a phrase like "perhaps one day" or "I'd like to" or "when the situation is right, I could." Take one of these forever ambitions and make a decision right now to either do it or get rid of it.

Exercise—Attach an action to it.

Now that you have made a decision, attach some form of action to it. The decision must change a thought from a wish to a serious commitment. When there is an action attached to a decision, it suddenly becomes real. That action is the beginning of the momentum that will lead you to accomplishing this goal.

Decision is not really a decision until there is an action attached to it.

When we make a decision, we gain power, focus, and direction found in no other way.

Determination is part of decision.

There is great power worthy of note in the familiar story of *The Little Engine That Could* by Watty Piper.

You'll remember the story focuses on a small locomotive that has to pull a big heavy load up a steep hill. While everyone around him told him he couldn't get the job done, he refused to believe it. Instead, the little engine tried with all his might. He pulled the heavy load as hard as he could. The entire time he repeated to himself aloud, "I think I can, I think I can, I think I can." The load was incredibly difficult, but he was determined. He did not give up.

Finally, after extensive effort, he reached the top of the mountain and began the easier descent down the other side. At the conclusion of the story, he had accomplished his task.

Life is often like that story! Those who are determined are able to do incredible things. They wade and trudge through incredible challenges, doubt, and scorn from onlookers. But as they push on, they eventually get to victory.

Success would be far more common if people would just learn this one principle of determination. Too many people try briefly, experience challenge, and throw up their hands, proclaiming, "It was never meant to be."

Recently I met a young man who was captain of his high school's track and field team. He was the city champion. As we spoke, he was about to go and race in the state finals. When I asked him what he did so that he could run so fast against other runners, he responded, "When I run, I just tell myself that 'I own this race. It is mine. I can do it. I will do it.' I am determined to run the race like I own it. No one can beat me when I think like that. It's not a matter of being the fastest. It's a matter of what I tell myself about the race and how hard I will let me push myself. No one's opinion matters except mine."

I have seen the opposite to also be true. When a person feels as though he or she is beaten, he or she slows down and eventually gives up. What will you tell yourself? Are you focused on the opinion of others? Are you determined to push yourself harder and faster than ever before?

Interested or committed?

There is a difference between interest and commitment. When you're interested in doing something, you do it only when circumstances permit. When you're committed to something, you do it no matter what.

Decision—Questions to consider

- What will I decide to do?
- What will I decide to let go of and will never do?
- How will this affect my future?
- What consequence will this have in the long run?
- What impact will it have on me and those around me?
- What action will I attach to this decision to get things started?
- Am I determined?
- What am I willing to do to show how determined I am?
- What will I do to stay determined?
- What do I tell myself about my goals?
- Am I listening to negative voices from the outside?
- What can I do to push myself just a little bit more?

Excerpts from the Success Interviews: Kelly Hrudey

Kelly Hrudey played for several years as an all-star goalie for the New York Islanders, Los Angeles Kings, and San Jose Sharks. Kelly is now a recognized expert on hockey, and he is a broadcaster on the TV show *Hockey Night in Canada*.

Doug: What does success mean to you? What is the definition of success?

Kelly: Success to me has to be setting your mind on a target. Having a goal and having a plan on how to get there. And making sure you have the right people around you to achieve that goal. Never letting anything get in your way. Nothing. Nothing can stop your plan. Not a roadblock. Not a detour. Not a naysayer. Never give in. Never give in. Never give in. Get the maximum out of your gifts and talents. That's just my way of thinking. And you will achieve something in the end.

Doug: What would you say has been the number one reason why you are successful?

Kelly: Without sounding like a complete idiot or egomaniac, I am successful because I never give up. Maybe that's dumb, but I'll never ever give up. I'll just keep trying and keep trying. And never give up. The idea that *you can't do it* or the word *no* just doesn't stop me. Never will. As an example of that, it might be interesting to know that I was a lousy goalie growing up in Edmonton as a kid. And I didn't ever play hockey to become a professional athlete. I never even thought about it. I never could ever envision myself being a pro athlete because I had no idea what pro athletes looked like or how they grew up or whatever. I had no basis for what they were.

But I just played hard and played as well as I could every single game. And I took losing extremely hard. Then it seemed like all of a sudden, I started to get better. And when I was about seventeen or eighteen, I think that was the point when I had an idea that this was something that might affect my life in a big way. And it did.

Doug: What has been the most challenging obstacle for you, and how did you overcome it?

Kelly: As a broadcaster, my shyness. That doesn't happen to be a very good trait when you are in the broadcasting industry. But I am and was, when I was growing up, a very good listener. I was able to hear a lot of things and become informed from other people about things. And this in turn helped to form my opinions. I think it's pretty safe to say that out of all the kids that went to school where I did, that I was the least likely to ever get into broadcasting. But I had a passion for it and a real interest in it. I just didn't know how to do it.

But once I was able to get into that sort of forum, it started to come a little more naturally than I ever would have expected. Having said that, though, I retain more of my shyness off camera than most people would expect. I am just a quiet normal guy. And I think that I have seen that with a lot of my broadcasting friends. It may seem odd. They are very good at what they do in front of the camera. But away from the studio, they are pretty normal, leaning more toward the shy side of things.

Doug: That is an interesting insight. I have also found that to be true. It seems that most of the larger-than-life and enthusiastic personalities that I have met are also quite shy. I hope that readers who might be shy will realize they are not different than a lot of successful people. And shyness should not keep them from achievement.

Kelly: When I was in Los Angeles, I was able to be around a bunch of movie stars and things like that. John Candy was a big hockey fan, and so he'd come to a lot of our games. And I had lunch with him one time before a game of golf, and I couldn't get over how quiet he was. He was an incredibly quiet person. He was very interested in your story and what you had going on. But I wouldn't say he was funny. He just had an amazing talent to be funny when he needed to be funny. The rest of the time, I think he was quiet too.

Doug: What do you do continually to stay successful?

Kelly: First off, I've never been the kind of guy to say, "Phew, I finally made it." My way of thinking would be, "I've met one challenge and now I'm going on to the next." And I continue to look ahead. I've never been one to look backward and say, "Wow, great job, Kelly. Mission accomplished." Instead, it's always been full steam ahead and then preparing for the next day and the next obstacle. My preparation has never changed. I only know how to prepare long-term and maintain myself in my industry to be important.

Doug: Share with us what you mean by that.

Kelly: In my industry it is very fickle. It's very narrow. My options are very narrow. I think that is what has always focused me. When I go back to my playing days, I was the number one goalie in Los Angeles all those years. And I had twenty-eight or twenty-nine backups along the way. By that I mean twenty-eight or twenty-nine guys trying to get my job. The wolf is always at the door in that occupation. And it is the same in broadcasting. There is always someone trying to get your job. I wouldn't blame them for wanting my job, for wanting to do what I do right now. I am on *Hockey Night in Canada*! I mean, that is the icon of sports television. And I would suspect there might be, and I am not exaggerating, thousands of broadcasters that would love to be in my position.

Doug: Not to mention the millions of fans that would love your job too.

Kelly: That's right. My mind-set is to continue to work hard and watch a ton of hockey so I can stay at the level where I am.

Doug: What advice would you give to someone wanting to be successful, whether in their business or their personal life?

Kelly: Believe in yourself and the people around you. You have to make sure you are around the right people who can support you. You can't do it all by yourself. You have got to surround yourself with people you can trust. And realize that they can support you and you can support them. Believe in yourself. Be positive too. People, I suppose, but I don't know many of them, could have success with a negative mind-set. But I don't know many people like that. Everybody that I know that has had success is a positive person. They believe in mankind and all the positive qualities in people. They don't look for the faults in people.

The Importance of *Now*

If not now, when?

I learned the importance of now in a very unique and memorable way I will never forget. I enjoy extreme sports, and not too long ago, I went white-water rafting with my brothers.

We went in the springtime, when the river waters are most high because of melting snow from the mountains. The river we chose for rafting was called Kicking Horse. It is one of the best-known rivers for white-water adventures in all of Western Canada.

For those who have experienced the Kicking Horse in the spring, you know how it got its name. It is a very turbulent river. The waves toss your raft every which way, and you end up getting very, very wet.

But that wasn't the most frightening part of our trip.

After the raging waves, we began drifting through a more calm part of the river. It was here that our guide invited us to row the raft over to the riverbank. As we stopped, he quickly hopped over the side of the raft onto dry ground and motioned for us to follow him. We did.

He was soon past the trees and climbing a small hill. The hill then turned much steeper into almost a vertical climb.

We followed him to the top, and then he stopped at the edge of a cliff.

"Who wants to jump?" he asked with a wide grin stretching across his face. He had caught us all off guard with the question. He asked again, "Who wants to jump?"

As we each peered over the edge of the cliff, we could see that it was a significant drop to the river below. We stepped back from the edge.

He smiled again, and we knew he was serious. "Who wants to jump?" This time my brothers began to joke that whoever jumped would certainly lose his life in the process.

I stepped back from the group and sat down on a log. I began to think about what a jump like that could mean. What would it be like? How would it feel? What would be the consequences? I began to imagine how it might play out. I thought of walking to the edge, looking over, and getting ready to jump. What would that be like?

I knew I would feel nervous and have tremendous butterflies beating around in my stomach. This would be a moment of decision. If I decided I could do it, I would have to break through those butterflies and just jump.

Still thinking in my mind about what it might be like, I imagined that I felt myself jump. I could feel the sensation of being in the air. I felt myself hit the cold water below. I imagined going under the water. I saw myself pop back up and then swim to the side. I felt a feeling of great satisfaction knowing that I had done it. It felt great to think that this was now a part of my life experience.

As I sat on the log, I then played out a second scenario in my mind. What would it be like if I didn't jump? I imagined approaching the edge and looking over to the water below. I also felt those butterflies of nervousness intensifying in my stomach. But this time, instead of jumping, I simply said, "No thanks," and then walked down the hill.

Then I thought what it would be like to watch all of my brothers jump from below. I reflected on the years to follow. What regrets would I feel for not jumping? I was pretty sure I could predict what would happen every time my brothers and I would meet at a family activity. They would point me out to their children and say, "There's the uncle that wouldn't jump." I would be labeled as a chicken. I would also know for the rest of my life that I was a chicken. I had faced a fear and said, "No thanks." The more I thought about it, the more I realized that I wanted a different life experience.

I recognized that the entire experience came down to just that moment of the butterflies. If I could get through that moment, I would have my experience.

So often in life, our greatest opportunities come down to one little moment. Not a moment in the past. The past is gone and we can't do anything about it. If we were the top salesperson in our office last week, it really doesn't affect our paycheck this week. If you were an all-star quarterback in high school, it doesn't make you a great husband today. What happened in the past is important because it's part of our experience. But what happened yesterday does not create a reality today or tomorrow.

This opportunity also did not come down to a moment in the future. The future is important. It is very crucial to have plans for the future and have a destination in mind. But the future is elusive, like the past. You cannot create a successful future by focusing exclusively on what is to come.

Rarely do our futures ever turn out exactly as we plan. And if we are waiting for the ideal future to arrive before we get involved, we will miss a lot of opportunities along the way.

The only moment we have any power over is the present. Right now. This second. Now is the only thing we have to work with in molding our future. It is only the moment of now that changes things. It is a fragile moment. If we ignore it, it disappears forever. As I sat on that log, I decided that I would take advantage of now.

I stood up and instantly rushed to the edge. I burst through my brothers and jumped. I didn't even wait for the butterflies. I just jumped. I had seized *now* and there was no turning back.

The fall happened exactly as I imagined, with a few slight variations. The water was far colder than I remembered, and immediately my body froze. When I resurfaced, I felt like an ice cube. I almost couldn't move, and the best swimming stroke I could do was the dog paddle. When I got to the side, I was choking up water. When I finally looked up, my brothers called down, "How was it?" I gave the best frozen thumbs-up I could manage and shouted back the lie, "It was awesome."

I was glad I did it even though it was terrifying. And then a funny moment of satisfaction came as they decided to walk down the hill.

As I sat there, I reflected on the importance of now. Some people have pointed out that when you spell the word *now* backward, it is the word *won*. That is really clever, and it is true you can't win unless you do something now. But it's more than just winning. Instead, I take each letter of the word *now* and say it this way:

NO

NOW = OTHER

WAY

If you want to be successful, there is *no other way*. You must take advantage of now. It's not just a matter of winning. It's the only way to create success. You can't accomplish anything, whether extremely successful or moderately successful, unless you take advantage of now. Failure to do so will keep you exactly where you are today.

If you are going to run in the marathon of life, now is the time to get involved. You cannot board a train once it has passed you by. Success requires you get busy doing something or you will simply lose the opportunity. Face that moment of butterflies and have the courage to jump right in and get involved.

A short time after I had the jump experience, a friend shared with me an interesting Zen proverb:

"Leap and the net will appear."

Too often we want things to be perfect before we decide to jump into something new. The reality is that the answers will never align perfectly. We need to act in faith and just trust that things will come together.

I have yet to meet a top achiever who had everything perfectly orchestrated before getting started. You need to leap in the moment of opportunity; there is no other way.

Exercise—Do it now.

Get up right now. That's right, put the book down. Do one thing right now that will lead you closer to your goal. Make a phone call? Send an e-mail? Go out and meet someone? It could be anything big or small. But get up and do it *now*. Now is the only moment you have to change the future. Don't let it slip away.

The importance of now—Questions to consider

What will I do right now?

Make a plan. In the future, how will I remind myself to take advantage of *now* opportunities?

How will I remind myself to be courageous?

What activities have I been putting off that can be done right now?

Visualization

What you see is what you get.

Extensive study and research have been done on the effects of visualization in the achievement process. The findings have been quite remarkable. So much so that many groups and individuals, from professional sports all the way to astronauts at NASA, have incorporated visualization into their essential training.

Visualization not only helps to prepare you mentally for an experience, but there are physical benefits as well. Studies have demonstrated that as athletes have practiced visualization, their muscle groups actually fire in the same sequence and order that they do in real-life experience.

As a result, the visualization experience was found to increase coordination and decrease reaction times. Visualization actually trains the brain to do things in a particular order, pattern, and level of effectiveness.

What is visualization?

Visualization is often described as precreating the success of an event in your mind. Most simply, visualization is described as seeing the end results of a goal as though it were already happening. This is a great beginning, but it is only partially accurate in describing what needs to be experienced in an effective visualization experience.

The process, not just the event

Stacey Chomyn is a world champion in karate and kickboxing. She has won gold medals for point fighting, and also for karate forms. The most remarkable thing about Stacey is that she is only twelve. Stacey attributes much of her success and confidence in competition to her ability to visualize positive outcomes prior to competition in real life.

She doesn't only form photographic pictures in her mind of the victory, but she tries to become emotionally attached. When visualization becomes emotionally charged, it takes on greater power. (See the next section, entitled Get Emotional.)

Studies have demonstrated that athletes, like Stacey, find it essential to imagine all the steps of the achievement along the way. Visualizing both the positive and negative aspects of the process are a necessary component. By being aware of the negative possibilities, we are also able to manage our expectations and prepare for the challenges that will come. These mental investments strengthen resolve and commitment to win.

In a competitive arena, such as sports, studies have also shown that an athlete's belief in his or her ability to perform is directly linked to his or her feelings of preparation. Visualization confirms and reaffirms that feeling of preparation.

Exercise—Visualize the complete experience.

When you visualize the complete experience, you are making a mental investment into the victory. The human brain is a peculiar computer. It has begun to calculate the price to obtain your goal even before you begin the first task.

Studies have shown that even when there is a quicker route to success, many people will sabotage themselves and search for a way to do more. This happens because of a principle in psychology called *investment bias*. Simply put, your mind needs to feel like it has invested time and effort equal to the reward before it will receive it.

Visualizing the complete experience teaches your brain that you have done the work and that you have prepared. It convinces your mind that you have made an investment and you are worthy to receive the end result. It tells your brain that it makes sense at this time for you to claim the prize of victory and achievement.

Visualize the entire experience (with emotionally charged and detailed realism).

To be effective, these five elements must be present in your visualization:

1) You must picture the entire experience, not just the end victory.
2) Include the investment of effort, pain, commitment, diligence, and learning to gain the victory.

3) These expectations must be as close to reality as possible.

4) The visualization must be emotionally charged. The more intense the emotional connection to the vision, the more realistic it will be to the mind.

5) Lastly, details must be considered. If you picture things in generalities, you will not receive the results that details acquire.

An additional consideration: Often a guide or coach can be very helpful in visualization exercises.

There is a story in the folklore of Walt Disney about visualization. Walt had such a clear vision of what his theme parks would look like that during construction, he could have discussions about details with the foremen without needing to consult blueprints. He just saw it so clearly that for certain aspects of the design, he didn't need to see the plans.

In visualization we must get to the detail. Try to consider each of your five senses: sight, smell, taste, touch, and sound.

The brain cannot tell the difference between experience and visualization.

I remember having a dream as a child about a chest full of toys in our house. I remember waking up and my mind believing the information so much that I actually spent most of the morning searching for the toys. Our mind cannot distinguish between real or imagined learning. The mind will treat vividly visualized experiences as though they are really happening in reality.

Visualization accelerates the learning process.

The studies that have been done on visualization have also provided some additional insights that I think are worthy of mention here:

- When the mind rehearses an experience, it is more confident when performing the same experience in reality.
- With continuous visualization, participants reported a significant increase in their belief and ability to succeed, and an increased desire to attain their visualized outcome.

- The visualization process enabled the participants to solve challenges and grasp concepts 40 percent faster than those who did not visualize.
- Those who visualized experiences were also able to complete tasks 30 to 40 percent more effectively on the first effort.
- People who visualized were able to create positive habits and break down negative addictions in a shorter time frame than those who did not practice visualization.

Visualization creates habits.

Habit comes through repetition. You have probably heard it said that habits typically take between twenty-eight and thirty days to develop. I conducted an experiment where I had ten of my coaching clients visualize a distinct new habit for twenty-eight days. They did not engage in the activity; they simply visualized it.

Ten days into the experiment, I began to see several of the participants demonstrate the character habit clearly. Fifteen days into the experiment, more than half were demonstrating clearly their new habit. And at the end of the twenty-eight days, it seemed as though nearly everyone had begun to act more in line with what I had asked them to visualize.

Conclusion: visualization translates into real-world behavior.

The postexperiment experience

My experiment also demonstrated that when the participants were asked to discontinue visualization, more than 50 percent had a decrease in those attributes and returned to their former selves. The lesson is that permanent work must be engaged in to create permanent results. I have found that this goes for visualization as much as it does for work in the real world.

If there is one thing I have learned through my interactions with top achievers, it is this: they are on a constant climb toward greater self-improvement. If we decide we have done enough and sit down to rest for too long, our lazier self will catch us and return us to our previous state.

Exercise—Solitude

Visualization requires time and concentration. Those two things are among the most significant obstacles to overcome for effective visualization.

Putting on a gentle piece of uplifting music will often help to keep your thoughts focused in the process. Journaling after the experience is valuable. If you know that you will be committing the experience to your journal afterward, it will be easier for you to maintain concentration. My study also confirmed that if you don't record your inspiration, you often don't remember it.

Exercise—Real-world visualization and recording it

Not too many years ago, I volunteered to do a session with Wayne Lee, a friend of mine who is a motivational hypnotist. I was curious more than anything to see what kind of techniques a hypnotist might use in visualization. I must admit I was a little skeptical at first, having never tried hypnotism. But after the session, I found I had really learned a lot.

When I left the session, I had a victory scene painted in my mind. I was emotionally attached to this scene, and even had a color assigned to that emotion as well. He did such an effective job that I found when I saw the particular color I had visualized later, I felt an immediate emotional reconnection back to the experience I had in the session.

I decided a great way to do that regularly would be to collect something to remind me of the color in the form of a sample card from the paint store. I keep that color swatch with me in my wallet and refer to it regularly.

I realized that there was a value in collecting other items I had visualized as well. I clipped out articles and saved ticket stubs, photographs, even fortunes from fortune cookies. They all went on my vision board and in my goal journal. They began to transfer the visualized world from my mind to tangible things that I could literally put in my hands. These tokens made my visualization more real. As your goals begin to become more real and intense, you will find more opportunities to act on them in the real world too.

Artistically and emotionally attached ▰▰▰▰▰▰▰▰▰▰▰▰▰▰▰▰▰▰▰▰▰▰▰▰▰▰▰▰

Emotional attachment to your visualization experience is essential. I saw a great example of how to do this when my wife and I visited the home of a family friend, Marlene Young. One day as we arrived at Marlene's house, she excitedly proclaimed, "It is done."

We followed her into her office, where she proudly displayed a painting she had completed. It was a painted image, but it had words as well. It described various feelings and victories in a colorful and powerful way. One of the first things I thought about was visualization.

Here was a significant emotional connection because Marlene had actually created it. Creation has with it a special magic and attachment of ownership. When Marlene had created this painting, she had experienced a great investment of herself and established a strong bond and meaning between the artwork and herself. The words and feelings in the painting had become vivid to her.

If you want to get really attached to your vision, create it in an artistic way. The artistic side of your brain is the portion from which emotion and creativity flow.

Don't worry about your artistic skill level; it won't affect activating the creative and emotional part of your brain. Just get artistic with your vision. By making this artistic connection, you will also establish a greater attachment to your vision of where you want to go.

Visualization—Questions to consider ▰▰▰▰▰▰▰▰▰▰▰▰▰▰▰▰▰▰▰▰▰▰▰▰▰▰▰▰

- What does the journey look like? Be specific.
- What does the destination look like? Be specific.
- What does this vision feel like? Be specific.
- What emotional attachments am I feeling?
- How can I intensify those feelings?
- Where will I set aside time to visualize each day?
- How am I recording my visualization?
- How can I turn my vision into real-life tokens?
- What can I do to artistically capture my vision?

Excerpts from the Success Interviews: Stacey Chomyn

Stacey is the under-twelve-years-of-age world champion for the World Kickboxing & Karate Association. That's right, I said twelve years old. You don't want to mess with her. She took Gold medals in two categories, and in the third category, Silver, at the 2009 World Karate championships in Orlando, Florida, at the Disney Epcot center. She was one of my favorite interviews because she calls it like it is.

We did this interview with Stacey a day after her thirteenth birthday, and I'm sure you'll agree her sport has given her experience and wisdom far beyond her years.

Doug: Hey, Stacey, it's good to chat again. How are you?

Stacey: I'm good.

Doug: So have you got karate practice later today?

Stacey: No, I had it yesterday, and I have it tomorrow. Today is my day off.

Doug: So how long have you been doing karate?

Stacey: I've been training karate for nine years.

Doug: You started when you were three?

Stacey: Yep.

Doug: So how did you know this was something you wanted to do?

Stacey: I got into it because my older sister started off in tae kwon do. We originally started off in tae kwon do. And then when we moved, we had to find a new club because I just wanted to keep doing it. My mom put me in a class and I really liked it. And she noticed I started doing better and better with it. It kind of kept growing on me.

Doug: Did you always know you wanted to do karate even as a little kid?

Stacey: I think so. I think I liked it because I could just be myself there and I could have fun while I was doing it. And it gave me confidence and basically it made me feel good. And just knowing that I could do it.

Doug: But it wasn't always fun.

Stacey: Not always. But that's when I'd have to remember the fun parts.

Doug: So how old are you right now?

Stacey: I turned thirteen yesterday.

Doug: That's right, your dad told me it was your birthday. Happy birthday!

Stacey: Thanks.

Doug: What would you say was the hardest part for you to become a world champ?

Stacey: Definitely the conditioning. If you weren't on your top game, you were in trouble. Learning the new techniques and remembering them. If you were in that ring and he called out a combination, you had to have it. You couldn't be like … "wait a minute; I need to think about this." Jab, cross, hook, kick. You had to know exactly.

Doug: So you needed to be 100 percent prepared.

Stacey: Yeah.

Doug: So what did you do to prepare yourself?

Stacey: At the time, I was doing four classes a week. And on Saturday, we went to the high school to do conditioning with a teacher that works there.

And then we went back to the dojo to do classes there. My dad would get me running on the treadmill, and we had a punching bag. So I would kick around the bag every night for a little bit. And eating. I had to cut back a whole lot. Because I had to lose five pounds because I was overweight. Yeah, lots of conditioning.

Doug: So how did you figure out the plan of what you needed to do?

Stacey: We would have group talks of how we would get ready for it. And our instructor would tell us all the things we needed to do and eat. He was a world champion.

Doug: So what was the hardest thing for you in getting ready?

Stacey:- Mentally and physically you had to get ready.

Doug: What did you do to get ready mentally?

Stacey: I would mainly daydream and see myself standing on that podium. I could see myself standing with the gold medals around my neck. I knew it was going to happen. I had such a strong belief. I knew I was just going to go in there and do my thing. I had to keep talking myself into it.

Doug: Some people call that visualization. How did you do it exactly?

Stacey: I would just kind of be sitting there thinking about it. A picture of me on the podium. And the two girls on either side as second and third. But me as number one, with my country flag hanging and all my medals.

Doug: Did someone teach you this technique, or did you come up with that on your own?

Stacey: My mom told me, "Now you just have to picture it in your mind. If you picture it in your mind, it will happen; I know it will." It was mostly positive energy that I had to move into my mind.

Doug: You really approach things as a very mature thirteen-year-old. I am really excited to hear about this exciting journey for you. What was the biggest challenge or roadblock for you once the competition started?

Stacey: I think at nationals I had a really deep thinking point. I got so nervous and I was freaking out. I couldn't even breathe. My mom took me aside, and I was so nervous, I was like ... underconfident. And so my mom took me aside and she was like, "You can do this." And my instructor came over and said, "Listen, Stacey, I know you got this. You are a good athlete. You are in good condition. Everyone has faith in you."

And then when I went in there, I ended up whooping everyone's butts and getting first. And then at worlds, I think it was, because there were fights before mine, I had doubts the very first night. I saw a lot of the older people going before me, and I was like, "Oh my God... Am I going to be in there doing that? I am in for a treat."

Doug: It was scary.

Stacey: Oh yeah. And when I got in there, it was a huge adrenaline rush, and I had to remind myself, breathe, breathe, breathe. Probably the scariest mental thing was getting myself in there and doing it. And believing.

Doug: That is tough, when you see someone in there and you know that you have to compete against them and they are really good. That can be scary. But you did have a lot of people there that believed in you. Do you think that made a difference?

Stacey: We had our own little section of people from Canada, and we would cheer each other on. Even if we were from different teams.

Doug: Team spirit and support is important. So if you had to give advice to someone competing in a sport—any sport; it doesn't have to be karate—what advice would you give them?

Stacey: To believe in yourself. Don't doubt yourself. If you don't believe, you're not going to go anywhere. And try hard. If you don't give it your all, you might as well just go home.

Doug: So what's next for Stacey?

Stacey: Well, I have my black belt test. And I'm going for that.

Doug: You're thirteen and you have your black belt test?

Stacey: Yeah.

Doug: That's pretty incredible.

Stacey: Thanks. And that's coming up really quick, in about two or three weeks. And I'm going to keep going. I'll definitely keep going. Maybe in a couple of years, I'll do worlds again.

Doug: Wow. That's great! Any other last thoughts you want to share with us?

Stacey: If you are ever having a bad day, don't just say, "That made me mad." Don't give up. Everybody has bad days sometimes. And if you don't get something right once, that doesn't necessarily mean that you'll never get it.

Doug: That's such an important thing. We all have difficult days in life. So when you had your really bad days, what did you do to keep yourself on target?

Stacey: Sometimes I would—me and my sisters, we are really close—we would hang out a lot, so I would sometimes just forget about it for a little bit. And have some fun or whatever, and then I would go back to it. It'll eventually come because practice makes perfect. I would talk with my teammates that I train with, and they would say, "Okay, let's go forward. You got this." I would pretty much keep practicing. And if I was having a bad day, my mom and dad were also really supportive.

Sometimes I would just leave it aside, and when I was calmed down or whatever, I would come back to it, and each time it would keep coming better and better.

Get Emotional

In dreams and love there are no impossibilities.
—Janos Arany

"Don't get so emotional!" Have you ever had someone tell you that at the end of a sad movie? Perhaps at a football game, where you got a little too loud? Maybe it was the day you finally got that raise at work? Or perhaps it was a negative situation and your frustration brought you to tears?

"Don't let them see you cry," is something we also hear, and in business we hear, "Never let them see you sweat." Emotion of any kind is thought to be a sign of fear or weakness.

I'm here to tell you that the opposite is true, at least on the inside. You need to get emotional about your goals. Thoughts and emotions go hand in hand. If you don't have emotions, you are a robot. And I have yet to meet a robot that has accomplished anything beyond what it was told.

If we are emotionally excited about something, that thing gets to be exciting to us. Emotional connections give us power. Thought and emotion are so closely related that William Shakespeare said, "There is nothing either good or bad, but thinking makes it so."

My friend Bob Doyle, whom many would know from the film *The Secret*, is considered a law of attraction expert. Bob suggests that it is important to think positive, but the real power doesn't come until we get emotionally attached to that desired result.

Ask yourself, "What can I do to get emotionally attached to the outcome I want?" Thinking is a valuable process, but until the process actually takes on deep emotional meaning, there will be no change in behavior. Sometimes people call this passion. I like that word. It makes sense to me as I consider certain events within my life.

One event in particular comes to mind. When I first decided I wanted to create the movie *The Opus*, I didn't have any of the pieces in place. I didn't have the complete financial resources, I had no commitments from speakers to participate, I had no film crew ... I had nothing. Well, almost nothing.

I had a committed emotionally deep vision of what I was trying to do. I had passion. As I shared this passionate vision with others, I could literally see excitement ignite others, and it was all because of my emotional enthusiasm.

Passion is contagious. Emotion can motivate yourself and others.

It has been said that enthusiasm is contagious. It is a fire that consumes all it touches, but I believe it is the same of other emotions as well. Including negative emotions. If you have ever been in the room with a grumpy, negative person, you know exactly what I mean. If we can learn to govern our emotions, we will have a great tool to help us share our vision with others.

There is an ancient prophet who once counseled his son that if he would be more successful, he should "bridle" his passions. I found it interesting that he did not advise him to extinguish his passions, but to bridle them.

Bridle means to guide or direct. If we bridle our passions or emotions, we can use them for appropriate activities—the same as you would bridle a horse to harness his power. If we pay close attention to our emotions and passions within ourselves, they will also guide us on a track to our greatest achievements.

What if I have no emotion?

If you have no emotion, then I'd suggest two possibilities:

1) You might be dead. Check your pulse. If that's fine, move on to 2.
2) You haven't found something you are truly passionate about.

When you have something you are truly passionate about, then you will become excited. If you are having a hard time finding the passion you need, begin by looking carefully at what you want and why you want it. Maybe take a quick visit back to the section on clarity to see if this end result is actually attached to a real need or want in your life. If there is no passion or excitement in your current situation, you might want to find something different to do.

American psychiatrist William James had a very peculiar insight on emotion. He stated, "Emotions are not created by thought analytics. Emotion is created through motion." In other words, we don't get to the height of our emotions through just sitting and thinking about it. (Although just sitting will create certain emotions—generally negative ones.) Useful positive emotion is created through motion.

The motion with which we conduct ourselves influences our moods and our feelings. If you are feeling depressed or discouraged, the first thing I want to invite you to do is to get up and get moving. Sitting on the couch in front of the TV just won't change things for you. But a walk, a jog, or a bike ride around the block will.

How we move controls much of how we feel.

Exercise—Get Emotional!

Do you really want to see how much effect your emotions can have on a specific situation? Try this. Next time you are faced with the task of inviting someone to a party at your home, try making your invitation in a less-than-enthusiastic way. Let the tone of your voice sound unexciting and bored. Talk slowly and disinterestedly. What will the results be? If you send forth invitations with those characteristics, you will soon find you are the only one at your party.

On the contrary, try to get some excitement in your invitation and become enthusiastic. You'll find that your success will follow the enthusiasm you approach your task with.

Get emotional—Questions to consider

- Why is emotion more powerful than just positive thoughts?
- What can I do to change my emotional state of mind immediately? What can I do to change my emotional state of mind right now?
- What activities can I choose to be more enthusiastic about?

4—What Will the Obstacles Be?

If you can find a path with no obstacles,
it probably doesn't lead anywhere.
—Frank A. Clark

You might be wondering why this section was placed before some of the others in this book. The reason is simple when you consider this little poem by Joseph Malines.

The Fence or the Ambulance

'Twas a dangerous cliff, as they freely confessed,
Though to walk near its crest was so pleasant,
But over its terrible edge there had slipped,
A duke and full many a peasant.
So the people said something would have to be done,
But their projects did not at all tally.
Some said, "Put a fence around the edge of the cliff,"
Some, "An ambulance down in the valley."
But the cry for the ambulance carried the day,
For it spread through the neighboring city,
A fence may be useful or not, it is true,
But each heart became moved with pity,
For those who slipped over that dangerous cliff;
And the dwellers on highway and alley
Gave pounds and gave pence not to put up a fence,
But an ambulance down in the valley.

Then an old sage remarked, "It's a marvel to me
That people give far more attention
To repairing the results than to stopping the cause,
When they'd much better aim at prevention.
Let us stop at its source all this hurt," cried he.
"Come, neighbors and friends, let us rally.
If the cliff we will fence, we might almost dispense
With the ambulance down in the valley."

Being prepared for an obstacle has its benefits. An ounce of prevention is much better than a pound of repair. Have you ever been helped by a first aid kit? I have. In fact, one year as my father, brothers, and I volunteered to help set up parade bleachers for a big event in our city, I fell off one of the top bleachers and ended up getting several stitches just to the side of my right eye. One of our friends helping out on the same project was a doctor, and he had a complete first aid kit in his van. Without leaving the location, he took me to the back of his van and stitched me up on the spot. He was prepared with everything needed to do the job.

One of the reasons he was so equipped is that he anticipated the kinds of problems he could run into. And because he was prepared, I was back to work within minutes of the accident. As we begin our goals, we can also prepare ourselves for potential problems. Can you imagine trying to climb Mount Everest without considering what the obstacles may be? You would discover quickly that you have to stop and get properly prepared.

Now of course there will be some problems we will never see coming. But there will be many problems we can foresee if we'll just use some of the tools available to us.

Success is to be measured not so much by the position that one
has reached in life as by the obstacles which he has overcome.
—Booker T. Washington

Puzzle seekers

Another reason I have chosen to place this chapter at this point in the book is somewhat more scientific. The human brain is wired to seek out patterns and establish order. That's why we love jigsaw puzzles or those crazy posters that you have to stare at for twenty minutes before you can see a picture. Our brain loves to sort out challenges. In some ways, it actually seeks them out. Here is where the danger to the achievement process appears.

Sometimes we allow our brain to create and establish problems and obstacles that do not exist. Sometimes we make things more difficult than they really are. Sometimes problems can be solved by simply changing your thinking about them and seeing them for what they really are.

Exercise—Overcoming obstacles with a team

Sometimes people think that whatever obstacles come their way, they are obligated to approach each one alone.

This is false. Some problems cannot be solved by a single person and require a team effort. You may find that with help from others, your obstacles are often more easily solved.

This exercise is divided into several parts. First identify the problems and then consider whom you might be able to go to for help. Who do you know that has attempted something similar and may be able to lend his or her expertise to identify potential obstacles? After you have identified your immediate experts, next expand your circle of helpers to also include those who have no experience with the problem. Often their unique perspective can provide effective answers that others may not have seen.

The next part of this exercise: discover how these people beat those particular obstacles as they were endeavoring to create a success similar to what you are attempting now. There is no rule book that states you cannot utilize the help and expertise of others in getting to your goals. Be sure to take advantage of the wisdom that others around you are willing to share.

As you begin the process of getting to your goals, try to keep in mind this insight from Henry Ford: "Obstacles are those frightful things you see when you take your eyes off your goal."

What will the obstacles be?—Questions to consider

- Where can I go to identify potential problems?
- Who can help me with some of these situations?

- Who might have a unique insight on my problem?
- What can I do to prevent some of the potential obstacles ahead of time?

What Are You Willing to Pay?

Everything worth owning has a price.

I remember as a young boy I rode my bicycle up the hill from my house to a little convenience store. This was a favorite place for my brothers and me growing up. As I went inside, I had selected a grape soda and a comic book.

When I went to the counter, the cashier told me that the total was $1.10. I now had a serious decision to make. I only had $1.00. What could I do? I was faced with a choice. I could not have both items.

Ultimately I left the soda and went home with the comic book. After explaining the situation to my dad, he put me to work raking leaves. I made the extra money and I went back for the grape soda.

There were two valuable lessons for me in this experience. The first lesson that day was that often in life, whatever we value most becomes our priority. For me that day it was the comic book. If you want to know what you value most in your life today, you can find it by looking at the kind of choices you are making. You are always making a sacrifice and leaving something behind to hang onto those things that you value most.

The second lesson I learned was that everything comes with a price, especially the attainment of your goals. What are you willing to pay? If you are willing to pay the appropriate price, you can have anything you are trying to achieve.

Some goals are like an auction.

In some ways, many goals are almost like being at an auction. Some of the most prized pieces have multiple bidders, and sometimes it can be quite competitive. While there is generally enough to go around for most things, some of the items up for bid do require you to do more than the average fellow. Sometimes the items available are rare and unique and can have only one buyer.

For example, if you want to be the top salesperson in your office, you have got to outsell everyone else. If you are striving for a gold medal, you have got to beat everyone else. There is only room for one person. There is no other way to do it.

If you aren't facing an outside competitor, you will have to face the one that is within you. You will have to call upon your greatest self to get to your highest successes.

While the price may not be entirely evident up front, there are certainly clues as to what things may cost. One of the best indicators is to find someone who has achieved what you want to do and observe what he or she had to do to get there.

The price will not be in terms of dollars and cents, although that may certainly be part of it. Most of the time the most expensive resource you will have to contribute is a commitment of your time, energy, and effort.

One of the most important considerations in regard to this cost is to make carefully sure that you are not sacrificing what matters most for something that matters least.

As an example, my value system strongly requires that nothing is more important than family. So things that would detract from that relationship and become a burden or expense for my family are often placed as less important. You must decide what your highest values are and determine how they will be affected by paying the price to get to your achievements.

Commit to pay.

When you know the expense of the achievement, it becomes a matter of diligent commitment to pay that price. As with the most expensive things in life, payments are often to be made in installments. Rarely are great successes accomplished in one sitting. In finance, the more regularly you make these installments, the faster you will pay the debt and the less interest you will pay. The same is true of achievement: if your installments are regular and of a substantial size, you will arrive at your goal more quickly. On the other hand, if your installments are sporadic and moderate, you may never arrive.

What are you willing to pay?—Questions to consider

- What am I willing to pay?
- Where can I find out what something costs?
- What have others who have attempted the same goals had to pay?
- What observable patterns can I duplicate?
- What will be the investment?
- How can I protect the things that matter most?

Expect to Fail

> Making your mark on the world is hard.
> If it were easy, everybody would do it. But it's not.
> It takes patience, it takes commitment,
> and it comes with plenty of failure along the way.
> The real test is not whether you avoid this failure, because you won't.
> It's whether you let it harden or shame you into inaction,
> or whether you learn from it; whether you choose to persevere.
> —Barack Obama

One of the most interesting things I have observed as I have conducted seminars throughout the world is a misunderstanding with relation to failure. Many people feel that failure is a terribly bad thing. When it comes to achievement, most people think they will either be incredibly successful or they will fail miserably.

These false expectations are the source of great frustrations for many. Frustration appears because the expectation is that success should have no setbacks and failure is perceived as a sign that you are doing it wrong. These thoughts are both false. Failure and success are not opposites at all. They are both checkpoints on the road to the same destination.

When you started to learn how to walk as a baby, you did not begin immediately by standing up and walking. You teetered and tottered and fell countless times. That is failure by definition if you consider the end goal to be walking. My parents didn't worry too much when I was a baby. Neither did yours. We fell and struggled to learn how to walk. Our parents knew that falling was a necessary part of the learning process. You would not have been able to learn how to walk without those efforts. As you continued to practice diligently after each of those falls and failures, you became more capable.

The process of achievement is similar. Anything you learn in life will be learned in the same way. At first you will struggle, stumble, and fall short of the goal. That is failure. As you persevere, you will ultimately grow in your capacity to perform the desired task, and you will be successful.

The problem with many people is that they quit before the skills are proficiently developed. Oftentimes they state that they have tried and it just didn't work out. How many times did they really try? How committed were they?

It helps to remember the commitment that a baby has in learning to walk. Babies have a drive that keeps them going even when they are afraid. True failure never really occurs until we quit.

The J curve

In education there is a term that describes this natural process of learning. It is called a J curve. The theory suggests that the way people learn is actually in the shape of a J.

They start at the bottom hook point on the J and initially, when they learn something new, they struggle and fail. You can see this reflected in the hook on the J sliding downward from the starting point.

Initially people struggle with new information and skills. But soon after, we see them begin to rise again, just like the stem along the back on the J. The only difference is that they have spent time struggling to learn the answers, or as some would say, getting into their groove; their progress is now rapid and dramatic. The stem on back of the J reaches up farther and farther past the point where the person began and continues upward without much resistance at all. Most lessons in life come to us that way. We initially struggle, and then we progress as we stay committed. That is a J curve.

Exercise—What are you expecting from your failure?

Often people find a way to accept failure, but they can't really see the lessons in it. They break past the initial disappointment of the failure but gain nothing in the process.

This happens because they are not expecting to gain value from the failure experience. Their goal is to leave the failure in the past, get up, and move away from it as fast as possible. It's easier to begin something new, rather than ask what went wrong. Asking what went wrong involves taking ownership, and that can be scary. As you experience failure ask, "What can I *expect* to learn from this experience? What will I do differently?"

Failure actually speeds you up.

Most people think of failure as limiting, and therefore they try to avoid it. But failure actually increases your speed. How can that be?

Simple. Failure is never a fall down. It's a fall up. Like when you are running up the stairs and you miss a step and fall. Have you ever run up the stairs and tripped? I have. That's falling up, and that's what failure really is.

When you attempt anything new without immediate success, you will always learn something. The lesson may be big or small. It may be as simple as noticing something that you didn't see before. Failure always has some benefit.

Everything you learn will increase your understanding and increase the probability that next time you attempt a similar problem, you will be better prepared. The initial slipup puts you in a better position to achieve success as you continue to try. Literally, when it comes to success, you will be slipping up the mountain.

Failure is not a detraction. It is a contributor. In fact, it is the contributing factor that ensures your success will be permanent. As you fail, you develop the personal attributes that will allow you to repeat the success and make it last.

Don't wait for risk-free.

While I advocate making smart decisions, I don't believe they need to be risk-free. Sometimes you just need to trust yourself and just get started. You can't plan or prepare for all the contingencies that might arise, so why bother thinking you can? Most of the big stuff you fear, you will never experience. Worrying about it will prevent you from getting to where you want to go.

The best rule is to learn what you can as best as you can quickly, then get started. You won't have all the answers. You won't be able to do the task perfectly the first time, and by waiting for perfection will never get anything done.

Top achievers are not perfectionists; they are improvisers. They trust that they can figure out many of the answers as they are moving forward. The majority of the answers come in the doing, not in the preparing. Most often they can't even be seen in the planning. Prepare the best you can, then get to work.

Perhaps the American inventor Thomas Edison said it best. When asked about why he wasn't discouraged for a lack of results he said, "Results? Why man, I have gotten lots of results! If I find 10,000 ways something doesn't work, I haven't failed. I am not discouraged, because every wrong attempt discarded is often a step forward."

Getting out of the boat before it reaches the shore

Many failures are from people who did not realize how close they were to success when they gave up. They invested extensive amounts of effort, time, and resources on the course, but then abandoned ship before any of that knowledge and experience could be put to use. Be sure that you recognize that a setback does not mean it's time to quit. Giving up is not a true conclusion. Often giving up causes you to wonder about whether you could have really done it. Sometimes those doubts can stay with you for a very long time.

Remember the movies.

I love movies. When I was in college, one of my favorite courses was my film analysis class. During my time in that class, I had a chance to see more than a hundred different movies. For nearly all of these movies, I was required to write a report on the story and structure of the film. As I did this, I began to notice certain formulas reappearing in the structure of the stories. Every story, for example, had conflict and challenge. You can't really have a story without them. But more remarkable than the presence of conflict was also where it occurred. In all of the great stories, the biggest challenges for the protagonist always came just before the final victory.

Life is often the very same way. So don't push pause on your adventure; keep going and what you may find in the next scene may pleasantly surprise you.

Expect to fail—Questions to consider

- What efforts have I quit too early and called failure?
- Where might I be on the J curve right now?
- What am I expecting from my failure?
- What have I learned from the failure that will benefit my future?
- How can this failure speed me up?
- What results have I gained that can be used to my benefit?
- If my life were a movie, what part of the film would this be?

Focus Is Key

Our life is what our thoughts make it.
—Marcus Aurelius

Have you ever stood in front of one of those posters where you have to stare to make the picture appear? Truthfully I've never seen one of those patterns emerge. I used to think people were just making it up to play a joke on me. But everyone reassures me there is a pattern there. I'm still not sure.

But one thing I do know is that the human brain is wired to look for patterns. We seek patterns so much that our mind creates pictures in clouds or in the flames of a campfire.

Searching for patterns is not unique to visual images. It can be seen in how we observe life situations as well. Sometimes we see things that don't exist just because our mind is looking for a pattern. One example of this is the phenomenon called the *halo effect.*

The *halo effect* was a theory proposed in the 1920s by psychologist Edward Thorndike. His theory was that if you strongly favored particular characteristics in an individual, you would overlook negative ones and actively seek out more evidence to support the positive attributes. You would continue to form a positive pattern, so to speak.

When in love people experience the halo effect by seeing only the positive attributes, putting on what some people call rose-colored glasses. Perhaps you've heard the saying that love is blind. After the courtship ends, people become more casual and intimately acquainted, and then they begin to see the imperfections they may have not been aware of previously.

The halo effect is a clear example that what we focus on, we will see.

The focus challenge

One of the biggest challenges with many people on the road to success is focus. They often overcommit and overburden themselves with things that do not matter or are not leading them to their destination. An essential element of keeping your focus is learning to say no.

It is important to learn to say no to things that are not leading you to where you want to go. These distractions may rob you of your time, energy, and resources. Be very selective to keep your commitments to a minimum and make certain that the commitments that you do make you keep.

Exercise—The problem telegram

To shift your focus from negative to positive, try this exercise. Take a piece of paper and write the problem or challenge you are facing at the top of the page. (Even writing down the challenge will provide you with valuable insights that will help you to see the problem for what it is.) After doing this, write down as many solutions as you can think of. Ask questions about what can move you closer to a resolution. List all of the options—even ones that may at first feel ridiculous to you.

After you have done this, begin to think outside yourself. Start writing solutions and advice that you think others would probably give to you. Make this part really fun, and imagine that you are getting this advice by telegram from prominent people in history. (For example, what would Abraham Lincoln tell me to do? Or what would Albert Einstein say about this? Or even Jesus.)

Then read through all the answers and determine which might serve you best. Recognize that your focus has changed from the paralyzing problem to proactive solutions. It won't take long until you will find something that can be done.

The main thing is to keep the main thing the main thing.

Focus is key—Questions to consider

- What is my focus?
- Do the priorities of my daily activities conform to this focus?
- How could I look at things differently?
- What typically breaks my focus?
- How will I keep focused?
- How will I keep my goals in front of me all the time?
- What will I do to keep myself excited about this goal?

Excerpts from the Success Interviews: LuAn Mitchell

Canada's number one female entrepreneur has led a life of inspiration. She went from being a pregnant teenage runaway to becoming the CEO of Mitchell Fine Foods. She is the author of the best-selling book *Paper Doll*. She currently hosts the radio show *Millionaire Mentor* on Voice America Radio. For more about LuAn, go to www.theLuanmitchell.com.

Doug: What does success mean to you? What is your definition of success?

LuAn: To be completely comfortable in my own skin in this life. So that in my past, my present, and my future and in this moment, every moment, I can accept myself and others and give gratitude for everything. And we can all grow together to make a better world.

Doug: What would you say has been the number one reason why you are successful?

LuAn: I am going to go right into the nuts and bolts of business. Because success in the perspective of the world leans heavily towards prosperity, that is, wealth creation, playing with the toys of life. I was literally born on the wrong side of the tracks, so according to the world at large, I didn't have the right number to dial up, but I was certainly able to dial it up and manifest it. Pretty much on every playing field I have ever decided to play on. I have always wanted to play hard for the team. And win. I didn't just want the brass ring. I wanted the gold or the platinum. And that's a part of me. You have got to believe that you deserve that and that others deserve that. I don't see why people can sometimes look at their own limitations and say that they were imposed on them. I don't have limitations. I have got to tell you, I never really dreamed of how fabulous it could be. If I want to go buy myself a new dress, I can do it.

Doug: What has been the most challenging obstacle for you, and how did you overcome it?

LuAn: My number one obstacle has been confusion, Doug. There have been times in my life where I can't help or postpone an uninvited pity party. Where I say, "Why me?" I know we never get more than we can handle. But sometimes it's like, "Whoa. My cup runneth over with this kind of thing." And I think *let's go look for another cup, or dump this one out already.* Because I think often we don't see things as they really are. There's a gift, I call it a seed for good, and it's in everything. I always tell people that there is good in everything difficult you may be doing. Find that, and the rest makes great fertilizer. But find that seed for good, and then you can bless that and plant it. If you can find that part in every situation, every person, and every difficulty, that will create the ultimate harvest for the entire world.

Fear vs. Failure

> One of the greatest discoveries a man makes,
> one of his great surprises, is to find he can do
> what he was afraid he couldn't do.
> ——Henry Ford

Fear and failure are not the same. But we often give them the same stopping power. Fear is the instinctive emotion aroused by impending or seeming danger, pain, or evil. In other words, fear is based on the future and what we imagine about it.

Failure is generally considered a result of not completing a task successfully. One definition of failure I found is quite interesting. Failure: to omit or forget to do something that is required for success.

Neither of these situations, fear or failure, is permanent. But both can have great power in preventing a person from accomplishing his or her goals.

Are you afraid of a man this big?

In school I remember children holding out their two fingers an inch apart in front of my eyes and asking, "Are you afraid of a man this big?" If I said no, then they would clap their hands directly in front of my face and make me jump back. Then they would say, "See, you are afraid."

Each time someone would come and try to play the same joke, I would focus on his or her fingers and wait for the big clap. As my friends and I played this joke on each other, we found ourselves staring longer and longer, waiting for the big clap to come. Sometimes it was a long time. Sometimes we would be so focused on those two little fingers an inch apart that no matter what was going on in the outside world around us, we would miss it. This is a lot like fear and worry.

If we have experienced something in the past, we sometimes worry that it will come again in the future. We often paralyze ourselves waiting for that clap to come. Most times in real life, it never does.

While in China I was invited to talk to a group of high school students about overcoming fears. I began the session by talking about how I used to catch small grass snakes in the forest near my home. I described how they were harmless and we used to pick them up with a stick and then throw them into a pillowcase for safekeeping. The students listened with excitement until I pulled out a pillowcase with something inside. Immediately they connected the pillowcase to the story I had just told.

I asked one of the students to help me by reaching inside and removing the contents. Inside I didn't have a snake, but several candy bars. No one would take me up on the offer to get a candy bar.

Often we link up things the same way. We create a fear or a problem where is none, just because there are similarities to situations we may have had challenges with in the past.

Breaking through conditioning may be difficult. Consider the famous experiments of Ivan Pavlov and his dogs. He conditioned the dogs to salivate at the ringing of a bell, even when there was no food present. He did this by linking the sound of a bell to the presence of the food. After this connection had been made between the bell and food for the dogs, he removed the food. The dogs still responded the same way to the ringing of the bell.

What bells are we responding to? There may be no snake in the bag. But often we see a bag and assume the worst. Sometimes the issues we fear are necessary for the delivery of what we really want, but our past experiences make those issues challenging for us.

The little things

Often it is not the big things that scare us. It is the little things or the things that do not exist at all. We become paralyzed by small things just because they are too close to our current vision. We choose to let them occupy our thinking, and significant opportunities are lost.

Procrastination can come because of worry.

Procrastination steals time, energy, relationships, possibility, and so much more. Studies have shown that procrastination is most frequently caused by either worry or laziness. The same studies have shown that most business opportunities are lost because of procrastination or worry.

Worry causes us to become paralyzed. We don't make any effort because we fear that whatever we do will have negative repercussions in some way. The longer and more consistently we feed the worry, the more powerful and controlling it becomes.

Exercise—What if vs. how can I?

When we give in to worry, we become paralyzed. To successfully break through these moments, list the worries that are bothering you on a sheet of paper. But don't just list them. Put them in their proper place. You can do this by beginning each worry phrase you write with the question "What if?"

Once you have your complete list, rewrite the list, but this time instead of putting "What if" at the beginning of the worry, put the words "How can I overcome or solve the problem?" So, for example, if you stated, "What if

I can't find the funding as I need it?" you would change that to "How can I find the funding as I need it?"

By shifting your thinking from "what if" to "how can I," you will find that you will also shift from becoming paralyzed to becoming energized by solutions and possibilities. The simple idea of finding a solution allows you to take control of the outcomes. Be a solutions-oriented person. Excuses and worry never built anything great. There will always be a way if you look at the situation with a "How can I?" perspective.

Exercise—What and why?

It is okay to be afraid of something. But don't just stop at the idea of being afraid. Ask what scares you about this situation and why. When we get specific about what it is we fear and why we fear it, we can begin to see the fear for exactly what it is.

With this perspective, we can then approach our fear with a greater confidence and resolve to succeed. Most of our fears come from what we don't know. When we don't know something, we often imagine the worst that we can dream up. Discovering the true origins of the fear and seeing it for what it really is takes away the power of that fear. It becomes powerless. In the light of day, this fear becomes quite manageable.

Here is one of my favorite thoughts from Theodore Roosevelt:

"In the battle of life, it is not the critic who counts; not the man who points out where the strong man stumbled or where the doer of the deed could have done better. The credit belongs to the man who is actually in the arena, whose face is marred by blood and sweat. Who strives valiantly, who does actually strive to do the deeds, and who falls short again and again because there is not effort without failure. Who knows the great vicissitudes, the great challenges and who, if he succeeds, knows the triumph of high achievement and who, if he fails, at least fails while daring greatly, so that his place shall never be among those cold and timid souls who never knew either victory or defeat."

A great definition of success is this: solving all the problems and fears between where you are and where you want to be.

When we understand our fears, we begin to have power over them.

Fear vs. Failure—Questions to consider

- What specific things am I allowing my fear to rob me of right now?
- What can I do right now that will turn one of my failures into a possible success?
- What things am I worrying about that may never happen?
- Will my worrying change anything in a productive way?
- How much time am I dedicating to worry versus creating a new and better situation?
- What things am I currently procrastinating about because of fear or laziness?
- What strategies will I utilize to overcome procrastination?
- What do I understand about my fears that gives me power over them?

5—Getting Started

What is not started today is never finished tomorrow.
—Johann Wolfgang von Goethe

Creating an Atmosphere of Growth

We can only create in life what we are and what we think about.
—Cyrus E. Dallin (a sculptor)

How do you use your time?

It has been pointed out that successful people and unsuccessful people have one thing in common. That thing is time. Everyone, no matter who you are, has twenty-four hours in a day. That's 1,440 minutes, or 86,400 seconds. We all have that in common.

Successful people invest their time in things that will provide long-lasting benefit and generate some kind of return. They look at their time as an investment.

On the other hand, less-successful people don't spend a lot of consideration in regard to their time. It passes without a plan or purpose, and often they run out of it before even getting to the important stuff.

One of the greatest thieves of time today is idle entertainment. Don't get me wrong, there are many wonderful ways to entertain yourself, and relaxation time is an important element in life. But too often we find people are allowing time-wasting entertainment to take more away from them than they realize.

What is time-wasting entertainment?

The most frequent kind of idle entertainment used to be considered the television. It has been estimated that the average person spends five hours in front of the television each day. ABC News once reported that children spend more time in front of the TV than in school or in sporting activities each day. The vast majority of that time is spent viewing programs that bring little or no value in exchange for the time invested.

For adults the numbers are similar—but rarely are the adults talked about. I guess we just expect more from our kids than we are willing to commit to ourselves.

What is watching television?

If you think about it, watching television is watching someone else live his or her dreams, and in the meantime sacrificing your own. Have you ever thought about this?

Popular youth speaker John Bytheway asked this question: "Did the people on TV ever come to watch me play basketball? Or accomplish my dreams? Did Jay Leno ever notice that you didn't tune in or send you a note asking where you were?"

Most of what is seen on the TV does not aid in successful thinking. In fact, it corrupts it. It paints a false view of what the world is and what the world has to offer. It also paints false expectations of what a life of money, excitement, and fame looks like. TV presents the dream but neglects to share the reality and the responsibility.

For years endless studies have demonstrated that the quality of what we put into our brains will directly affect how our brain is able to function and process any new information it receives. Most of the idle TV content during the prime-time hours offers very little that is constructive. Have you seen these statics? The top five activities most frequently portrayed on prime-time television today are:

1) Murder
2) Adultery or irresponsible sexual conduct
3) Criminal activities (including drug use)

4) Family breakdown/crisis
5) Criticism of individuals or organizations

These are certainly not common attributes in the lives of the most successful people in the world. Why would you want these thoughts nurtured regularly in your life? You've probably heard the saying that good input equals good output. And bad input equals bad output. I don't think it is much of a coincidence that the most successful people whom I have met in the world choose to dedicate little time to watching TV. (You may this interesting: that also includes the celebrities who make a living appearing on TV.)

Here's another interesting thought: the *Journal of the American Medical Association* found direct links between excessive TV viewing to eating disorders, obesity, smoking in youths, drug use in youths, and a direct increase in violence. Excessive TV will have negative effects. Even if you aren't affected to these extreme levels, remember that it is impossible to touch wet paint and not get some on your finger.

If you can eliminate some of your idle TV time and dedicate it to something worthwhile, you will see many of your results immediately change.

Exercise—How much did it cost?

Oftentimes we flick on the TV and sit down without thinking. We watch a few shows and time passes quickly. For the next week, chart how much time you are spending in front of the TV. When you have the final figures, consider what you could have accomplished in the same amount of time.

Are you a net junkie?

The Internet has been taking over in many lives. Most experts feel that it has even overtaken television as number one for idle entertainment. Chat rooms, online gaming, and aimlessly surfing are currently robbing businesses, employers, and individuals of precious time. People are becoming net junkies.

Countless hours and opportunities are lost, never to be seen again.

What were they exchanged for? A dragon conquered? A game level passed? Chitchat without purpose?

Take a look at your current activities and determine what you are trading your most valuable resource, your time, to get.

Relationships in the real world are essential to success.

In the real world, relationships with people are always a key component of creating success. You cannot connect as effectively when you are isolated at home. Even business relationships that start online need to shift offline to be totally effective. Creating an atmosphere of growth in this area includes finding activities that will stretch your mind, create relationships, and help you to gain skills that will make you the best you can be.

Get up early and get to bed at a reasonable time.

Studies have shown that those who rise early and get to bed at reasonable times have greater thinking and creative ability. A brain that is fatigued does not perform at full potential. What time are you getting to bed and waking up?

From my research of the most successful people, it was discovered that their most productive hours were before 11:00 a.m. The day typically began at 5:30 or 6:00 a.m. for many of them. The morning included personal studies or routines that they had created for personal growth. Then they took their most important meetings in the mornings and had the afternoon to complete items determined in those meetings.

> Early to bed and early to rise,
> makes a man healthy, wealthy, and wise.
> —Benjamin Franklin

Creating an atmosphere of growth – Questions to consider

- How am I using my time?
- What can I do to chart my use of time?
- What can I do to make my use of time more effective?

- What surrounds me that is not adding to my success?
- What things around me are robbing me of opportunities?
- What boundaries will I establish for myself concerning exposure to time-wasting entertainment?
- What good input can I find to put into my life?
- What can I do to create more valuable relationships in my life?

Make a Plan

*In preparing for battle I have always found that plans
are useless, but planning is indispensable.*
—Dwight D. Eisenhower

Plans are often defined as a blueprint or map to get to a destination or to complete a project. Yet experience demonstrates that life rarely goes according to plan. It is not uncommon to hear the following questions or concerns about planning:

- *I don't want to set a plan because things will change anyway.*
- *I can't see far enough ahead to know what I should include in my plan.*
- *What happens if I want to change my plan?*
- *While working on my plan, I found that I've changed my mind about what I want to do.*

Plans for creating success and getting to goals differ in many ways from plans that are used to create buildings or bridges. Plans for creating static nonliving items can be built predictably and precisely. They can be built in such a way that quantities, checkpoints, requirements, and results can all be counted on. But with living organisms like people, things will change and must be adaptable.

Plans for goal setting and achievement are less like maps for cars to follow or blueprint plans to build something. Success plans are more like receiving a direction and a compass. We know where we are headed and we can use these tools to stay on course, but the course may or may not follow a particular outlined path.

The gift of careful planning is structure. ~~~~~~

While exact planning will never work in goal accomplishment, careful planning can help to give you structure.

When I worked on the movie *The Opus*, I utilized planning to my greatest advantage by creating a workable structure. I shot some of the film at the San Diego convention of the National Speakers Association. I knew that some of the speakers I wanted for the film would be in attendance at that event. Some of the speakers I had never met and I didn't have a commitment from them to participate. But I wanted to include them.

I knew I would only have a brief moment for them to grasp the vision of what I was trying to do. So I made a plan of how I might make contact with them and more specifically what I would say. I made a plan with my camera crew as to what needed to be done so they would be ready, and I prepared a shooting schedule that could accommodate the filming for these sought-after speakers if I could add them. This was all structure. Most of the variables I was dealing with were unpredictable and not planned. When I got to the event, I talked with people about where I might find the speakers I was seeking and made arrangements to be in those places.

As a result of this kind of planning, I was able to be ready for the speakers who said yes. I was able to include in our shooting schedule Jack Canfield, Mark Victor Hansen, Dr. Joe Vitale, Marci Shimoff, Willie Jolley, Ed Tate, and others. Planning for structure was a necessary component of preparation.

Of course, not everything went according to plan. There were others whom we missed, and some things that didn't go as smoothly as we'd hoped for. But we were in a much better position because of our structured preparation to maximize our effectiveness.

Exercise—Make a workable plan. ~~~~~~

In goal setting, a workable plan does not have every point outlined in great detail, but it should have some of the significant stops and checkpoints outlined along the way. The plan needs to include things that are considered absolutely crucial and essential to accomplishing your particular goal. To have an effective plan, include things that you can control. With the above example, I could plan what I would say to a speaker for my film, but I could not control whether he or she would listen to me or agree to participate.

When creating a workable plan, it is a good idea to include all who are involved. They may have insights or solutions to increase the probability of your plan being successful.

Make a list of things you know for certain that you will need to do in order to accomplish your goal. List these things in the most likely chronological order of how they may occur. Once you have your list, brainstorm what you can do to accomplish each one of those items.

After reviewing these needs, create the plan by orchestrating specific action steps. Start with what you can do today. No plan is of value unless it can be implemented into action.

Exercise—Make a plan each day.

It is easy to get lost in a big plan. Most entrepreneurs get lost in day-to-day activities after building a business plan that is for five years or more. It will always be the daily activities that require your attention first. Once daily activities have structure, you will be more relaxed to deal with the big picture. Set daily goals or plans on how you will get to those big goals. Try to limit this plan to a few workable and manageable tasks that provide the most benefit in working toward your goals. Prioritize these activities in terms of which activities are going to be the most valuable to you.

Carry this plan or list with you throughout the day and focus your efforts on what you can do today on that list. Much time is wasted worrying about the bigger picture. The big picture will come into focus as you zero in on what you can do now and get busy doing it.

Make a plan—Questions to consider

- What elements can I include in my plan today?
- Where can I go to find the essential steps to include in my plan?
- What action steps will I take on my plan today?
- How will my plans help me prepare to take advantage of opportunities as they become available?

Where Are You Starting from?

Your beginning is just as important as your ending.
You need both to understand where you are.

West Edmonton Mall is the world's biggest shopping mall. There are hundreds of stores, a water park, a hotel, an amusement park, a sea lion show, a skating rink, movie theaters, several food courts, and dozens of other attractions scattered throughout.

It is not hard to become lost in this mall, and one time my family and I were. The only way we were able to find ourselves was to consult the large map of the complex. Before we could determine where we needed to go, we had to find out where we were. We did this by locating the big red sticker that shouted out, "You are here!"

With the starting point and the final destination figured out, things were relatively easy. The same is true in the achievement process. You need to know where you are and where you are going to make every step count.

You might be closer than you think.

As I have worked with hundreds of individuals and companies in my coaching programs, I have been surprised to discover how close many people actually are to their goals before they begin. The lives they have led up until now have put many pieces into place that can be immediately adapted toward creating the results they are looking for. But often without help from the outside, they cannot see it.

You can't see the picture when you're inside the frame.

Often they are very close to the goal, but they just can't see where they are in relation to it or the resources they have already accumulated that could contribute. It might be in the form of the people they have relationships with, their education and experience, or even places they are traveling to on unrelated business that gives them access to some of the most powerful opportunities to build relationships with key people who can help them.

Exercise—Take an inventory.

When working with my students, I begin with a brainstorming exercise. On a piece of paper, we write the goal in the center. We then answer the following questions:

- What tools do you already have in place?
- Who do you know that can help you?
- What skills or education do you already have that can help you get to this goal?
- What talents do those around you have that you can draw upon to help create the accomplishment of your goal?
- Where have you been?
- Where will you go?
- Who will you meet?
- Whom have you met recently that can help?

Often it helps to ask the following questions about what you need as well. By asking what it is you need and seeing the answer, you may also be able to recognize how certain aspects of your life may already provide the answer.

- What tools do you still need?
- Who would be best to know that could help?
- What skills or education would you need to accomplish the goal?
- What talents would you need?
- What kind of person could help with this goal?

When you have completed an inventory of what resources are available to you, consider how you might best position what you have to help you. Remember that it is not necessary to have all the answers. As I said earlier, top achievers are not perfectionists; they are improvisers. The balance of the answers will come as you continue to move closer and closer to the accomplishment of the goal.

Through this exercise you will also be able to identify key skills that you will need that perhaps you do not yet have. When you identify these skills, you can then consider where you can go and find someone who can either help you with those skills or teach them to you.

Gratitude

Being grateful for the aspects of this goal that you already have in place or have access to will give an immediate boost in your momentum to get there. Gratitude expands whatever it touches. If you are grateful for progress you have already made and recognize what you have, it will expand.

Where are you starting from?—Questions to consider

- What do I already understand about this goal that I may have learned elsewhere?
- What experiences have I had that can be used to help me with the accomplishment of this goal?
- Whom do I know that can help me get to this goal?
- What tools do I have today that can be used to accomplish my goal?
- What new skills will I need for the accomplishment of this goal?
- Where can I find someone who can help me with those skills?

What Can You Do Right Now?

By the yard it's hard, by the inch it's a cinch.
—Unknown

One hot summer day my fifteen-year-old son Jordan exclaimed, "I am so hot I could drink ten glasses of water." I told him I didn't think he could do it. He insisted that he could. So together we went into the house and agreed upon the size of the glass and then lined up ten full glasses of water. Jordan sat down at the table and he started.

After a sprinting start, he got through three and a half glasses and then stopped. We both knew at that moment that he would have trouble finishing all ten. He smiled, looked at the glasses, and asked, "Is there a time limit?"

Jordan did finish the glasses of water. It took a lot longer than expected, but he did it. When we approach a glass of water, one or two might be refreshing, but too much water at one time is too much. It could prove fatal and even drown a person.

Since then I have thought about this in relation to achievement. Often we try to take on far too much more than what is comfortable. When we do, we become overwhelmed and then quit.

The problem wasn't that the goal was not attainable. The concern comes down to creating the right size of task along the way so that we are not overwhelmed in one sitting. Start with what you can do, and little by little you will create something incredible.

Exercise—Not what you could do, but what you can do.

One of the greatest gifts you can give yourself this instant is to forget about the things you *could* do, and focus on the things you *can* do right now. Then get busy and do them.

Make a list of the things that are within your power right now and then get started.

Getting started creates momentum.

Getting started even on the smallest tasks starts the momentum that you will need to get going with the bigger things. As you develop a deeper investment into your goal, your resolve to keep investing will grow stronger and the finish line will become real.

Exercise—Break it down.

Often we look at the enormous nature of a task and become intimidated. It is easier to walk away thinking that someone else may be better suited to take advantage of that opportunity. Many great and grand opportunities have been lost that way.

As a boy I learned a valuable lesson working with my father. One Saturday he took my brother Jamie and me out to work on a project with him for an elderly lady in our community. Part of this job required us to move a large pile of dirt that had been dropped on the front lawn. When I first saw the pile of dirt, I was worried because it was taller than I was. I had no idea how we could possibly expect to do such a job.

When I asked my dad about it, he simply replied to start one shovel and one wheelbarrow at a time. That was manageable. I could see how that would work. We began, and by midafternoon, much of that pile was gone. And by the end of the day, you wouldn't have even known a mountain of dirt had been there.

When faced with a task of gargantuan size, break it down into what you can handle. Ask, "How can I find in this task a simple step that I can do now?" And then get started.

Turn your could-do efforts to can-do accomplishments.

What can you do right now? —Questions to consider

- What can I do right now?
- What could-do things are keeping me from getting started?
- What larger tasks could I break down into smaller more manageable tasks?
- What is the smallest thing I could accomplish today that would get me started?

Regular Commitment

One person with commitment is worth more than
a thousand people who have only an interest.
—Unknown

Commitment and continued effort are the only true ways to build success. Lack of commitment is the most common reason why people fail. It's as simple as that.

Johann Wolfgang von Goethe said, "Until one is committed there is a hesitancy, the chance to draw back, which always leads to ineffectiveness. Concerning all acts of initiative there is one elementary truth, the ignorance of which kills countless ideas and splendid plans; the moment one definitely commits oneself, then providence moves too. All sorts of things occur to help one that would otherwise never have occurred."

Commitment indicates your level of performance.

Commitment is a standard or level of performance. The most successful people have a high standard of performance. They will not shrink from excellence to create something mediocre. They understand that mediocre efforts in one area will find reflection in mediocre results somewhere else in their life. There is a great truth to the saying that "If something is worth doing, it is worth doing right." That is not to say that things need to be perfect. All things should be done well and with the best efforts possible, though.

Perhaps you have also heard, "Anything worth doing well is worth doing poorly at first." Life is a learning process, and everything we do we will do poorly at first. Do you remember the first time you tried to ride a two-wheeled bicycle? No doubt you awkwardly wobbled back and forth. You probably even fell down a number of times. But eventually you got better, and today you are probably quite good. It all came, not because you were perfect, but because you did your best. In life we always go from poor to proficient. If we practice enough, we will eventually wind up a professional. We cannot let fear or embarrassment rob of us of the opportunity to develop a skill that could open the doors to success in the future.

Practice increases your ability to learn.

A friend of mine speaks seven languages fluently, and when I asked him how he did it, he stated that, "Learning the first few languages was hard, but once I spoke three languages, the rules for acquiring new languages were clear to me and the others came easier." Once we learn how to learn, it becomes even easier for us to learn. But the learning begins only as we stay committed.

Is commitment a sacrifice?

Commitment is more than just a verbal declaration of involvement or interest. It requires that you actually make a dedicated effort to get something done.

Commitment means that a significant sacrifice is required. Be sure that you are aware of what you will be getting for the price you are paying. Will the price you will be required to pay provide the results that you are seeking?

If what you are seeking is valuable and builds you into a better person, you can safely assume that the effort is not a sacrifice at all. The investment will pay far larger dividends than you would have imagined possible.

A final thought on commitment

Many people begin with great ideas and opportunities. However, when things get difficult or don't run smoothly, they abandon the dream. Top achievers are committed, and abandonment is not an option.

Exercise—Coaches for commitment

Find a person whom you can check in with to help you keep committed to your goal. Ask him or her to help you remember why you wanted this goal in the first place and what motivated you to get started. Arrange regular appointments for him or her to follow up on what steps you are taking to accomplish your goals. (You can find excellent coaching tools and support through my Sales Success Pilot program. You can find more information at www.TheSalesTrainer.com)

Exercise—Draw the time line.

Take some time to map out the time line of what you have already invested in this goal so far. Carefully ask yourself what you have done and what still needs to be done. Chances are you will surprise yourself with how much you have already accomplished and how close you may actually be to the finish line.

Exercise—Make a promise.

My friend Bill Bartmann doesn't like to use the word *goals*. He prefers instead to use the word *promise*. "People," he explained to me, "will often break their goals and resolutions, but no one likes to break a promise." When we make promises to get committed and get things done, things begin to happen differently. We must be careful to make our promises sparingly and guard those commitments as sacred.

Regular commitment—Questions to consider

- What will I commit to do?
- When will I do it?
- What will be the penalty for broken commitments?
- What will be the reward for commitments kept?
- What experts can I consult to make sure my commitment is moving in the right direction?
- What is my standard of excellence?
- What skill can I practice more carefully to get better right now?
- Do I have experts helping me to stay on target with my commitment?

What Are You Going to Do about It?

Performance is your reality. Forget everything else.
——Harold S. Green

Imagine a football team huddling on the field discussing a plan for gaining several yards and making the winning touchdown. How surprising would it be if as they concluded their plans, they walked directly off the field to sit at the bench rather than stay on the field and play? Of course, it would be absurd.

This may be one of the most important sections in this entire book. As I have researched success, I have found that one of the most incredible lies that people believe is that results can come without effort. Everyone is looking for instant success. I have yet to find a successful person on the planet who has achieved success without a great amount of dedication and hard work. There is yet to be a best-selling book that someone did not sit down to write. There has yet to be an Olympian who has received a gold medal who has not trained. There has yet to be a successful businessman who has not invested effort to make his business run smoothly. The list could go on. The truth remains: hard work is required.

Some people like to talk about great things; successful people get up and do them. Work is the only thing that changes your current situation. Work is the only thing that gives you true ownership of your accomplishments. Without work, a dream will never be realized.

Specific actions will get specific results.

Action must be done with clear purpose. The more carefully you place your efforts in the things that matter most, the more effective your actions will be. It is not a matter of getting busy. It is a matter of getting busy with the right things.

Do it!

The title of this section may be a little too obvious. Is it necessary to tell people to do it? Experience has shown that this is one of the most neglected areas of the entire achievement process. Too often people come to a seminar or read a book and they are instantly motivated. There is no question that they enjoyed their time at the event and great information was exchanged, but for many that's where it ends. The books they purchase become shelf help instead of self-help.

Perhaps you have heard the famous saying, "Give a man a fish and he eats for a day. Teach a man to fish and he eats for life." It is a saying that is only partially true. If you teach a man to fish, there is no guarantee he will use the information. For all we know, he may just sit in the classroom and learn about fish all day. What he needs to do is apply that knowledge by getting himself to the lake or river and starting fishing.

Action in the right way and the right place arise the only thing that makes a difference. Knowledge alone will not do it. Good intentions will never pay the bills. Good intentions are necessary. They are the beginning. But where intention turns to action is where successful and less-successful people are separated. The best way to get something done is to do it. It's as simple as that.

Two types of people

People can be separated into two columns. Some have suggested that these two columns should be dreamers and doers. This is not true. We are all dreamers. The two columns are doers and those who do nothing. Doers pursue their dreams and in that process create amazing results in their lives. Non-doers or even partial-doers create nothing because they do nothing. Which group will you belong to? The only thing that will determine which group you belong to is found in what you will do. Not in what you dream about. What will you do about your dreams to turn them into reality?

What are you going to do about it —Questions to consider

- What will I do to get started now?
- How hard am I willing to work to make this goal happen?
- What kind of work will be the most effective?
- How soon will I implement what I have learned?
- What situations have most recently passed where this information would have helped?
- What plans could I make for the future that would ensure the information is used?

Overcoming Procrastination

*Procrastination has caused more damage
to the human race than any disease.*

Procrastination and excuses

It has been said that the road to hell is paved with good intentions. Here's some news for you. So is the road to heaven. The only difference is that those on the road to heaven actually did something with those intentions. They did not just dream away their time. They did something by taking advantage of the moment. Remember that procrastination and excuses never created anything.

What is procrastination?

Procrastination and excuses are expressions of either fear or laziness. If you are afraid, you can find courage. You just need to do it. Bust through the butterflies and it will all work out. The Chinese philosopher Tao Te Ching said that, "We become brave for that which we love." If we truly love and desire our goals, we will find courage to exceed the fears we will face. Any time you are attempting something beyond what you already are or have, there will be some degree of fear.

If you are lazy, there is not much anyone can do for you. Your future will always be the same until you decide to get to work.

Procrastination is a thief.

It has been said that procrastination is the greatest thief of all time. This is true literally because procrastination steals time. When time goes, opportunity goes with it. In the end, *one* of these days eventually becomes *none* of these days. The things that we put off eventually become the things we never get the opportunity to do at all.

Procrastination occurs when there is no motivation.

Typically procrastination occurs because we haven't placed a high enough value on a task to acquire the motivation to get it done. The nature of the activity doesn't really matter. My studies conclude that people procrastinate easy things just as often as hard things.

If you are encountering procrastination in getting to your goals, this might be a good time to go back and review the section Get Clarity. If you have lost sight of why you started toward your goal or your why has lost its meaning, then you may need to reevaluate if this goal was really what you wanted in the first place. And if it was, then it's time to dig deeper and find more reasons why to charge up your personal motivation to get going.

Too much fun can hurt too.

Fun is not a bad thing. But if you are procrastinating what needs to get done because you are choosing to do the fun things or easy things of life instead, you are being robbed of your potential.

We often let things we really enjoy creep in and take us off course: The buddies want to go play golf that afternoon, maybe a new movie is out, or the big one that so many people are falling into now, video games and the Internet or chat/social groups online. It could also be something even more camouflaged than that. Sometimes we procrastinate essential work to do less meaningful work just because it's easier.

Consider this: If a beautiful girl (or for the ladies, a handsome hunk) came and held a gun to rob you, would it still be considered robbery? Of course it would be. It probably wouldn't feel as threatening, but you'd still be there with an empty wallet.

In fact, most often it is the little things that we delight in that rob us of our possibilities. Those things are harder to say no to. Just because an activity seems fun or entertaining, we need to determine that we won't let it become a distraction to us. We must learn to prioritize the most important things to take up our most valuable energies.

Exercise—Schedule it!

Quite frankly I am not 100 percent against procrastination or taking a break to be lazy and do nothing. These things have their place, and I like to do it sometimes myself. Where procrastination becomes a danger is when it replaces an important task and interrupts your effectiveness. Important necessities need to come first, and success cannot be attained if they are left to find second place to procrastination.

Here's something you might want to try. When you are tempted to procrastinate, schedule it. Literally pull out your planner and block out a space of time to do nothing. Just make sure that you put it after things that are most important.

Exercise—Set up a border.

A useful exercise that has allowed many to become more effective has been to set up specific borders while doing your work. Set up a time where you will allow no distractions, phone calls, visits, or e-mails. During that time, focus on nothing but the task you have chosen for that moment. You can proceed through your work without anything to slow you down. Generally the best time is early in the morning. That way if you want to do something fun and nonproductive with friends, you are ready when they are.

Procrastination saps energy.

When we procrastinate, we also lose momentum, energy, and excitement to get to our goals. American psychologist William James observed this when he said, "Nothing is so fatiguing as the eternal hanging on of an uncompleted task."

Remember that time passes regardless of what you do.
Tomorrow you will wish you had started today.

Overcoming procrastination—Questions to consider

- What am I trading my most useful time for?
- When is my most productive time?
- What activities most often get in the way of my productivity?
- How can I build an escape route to keep me on task?
- What borders can I establish to keep distractions away?

Excerpts from the Success Interviews:
Ken Pattenden is the President of Taco Time Canada.

Doug: What are the most important attributes successful people need to have today?

Ken: Perseverance and determination. There is nothing that is easy. If you have a good idea, you better have the fortitude to be able to keep pushing it through, because things are just tough to get done.

Doug: What is the biggest challenge to your success?

Ken: The biggest challenge? Probably getting people to buy into my ideas and level of commitment to a project. That's probably the biggest challenge. Whether it's finance or someone to execute the idea, the people that you need, whether they are employees or lenders, whatever it is, you'd better have a real heart-to-heart to see whether they really have the same kind of commitment to the execution of the project as you do. And if they don't, you've got to find the right people before you get too far down the path. What you don't want is to get halfway down the path and find that somebody's goals are not the same as yours.

Doug: Do you mean surrounding yourself with like-minded people?

Ken: Well, not so much like-minded people. Sharing the same goal. I think that's different than like-minded people. You don't necessarily need a bunch of type-A people sitting around a boardroom trying to get something executed. You need different types of people—who all need to know what the goal is. I think getting them to understand that is important.

Doug: What is the best advice you can give to someone in pursuing a goal?

Ken: Keep the faith. If you believe it is right, make it right. Don't second-guess yourself. It really goes back to the perseverance. It is really important when you do a check halfway through your performance that you are really heading in the same direction as when you started.

Doug: What has been the biggest help to you in attaining your goals?

Ken: Trying to keep the broad perspective of what the goal is. And throughout the task, try and make sure that you don't get too mired down in the details of it without remembering what the goal was. You need to be able to separate yourself a little bit from things to be able to remember what the goal was.

Doug: What is your definition of success?

Ken: Accomplishing what you set out to do. That really can be in anything. Getting it done.

Involve Others

Mount Everest could never be climbed by a single individual.
Some things are just so large they require a team to get them done.

Mentors

Have you ever seen a race car zipping around a racetrack? Imagine when it came time for the driver to pull into the pit stop that there was no one to help him. How long would it take if he had to climb out of the car and change his own tires? Or service his own engine? Or fill his own gas tank? Would it slow down his race time significantly?

Professional pit crews are typically done in a matter of seconds. But if a racer had to do the same tasks alone, he would be there for many minutes. The same thing happens for people trying to get to their goals alone.

Where can you get help?

One of the most important things you can do to keep momentum as you strive to accomplish your goals is to consider who can help you. The experience and support of others will help you to be more effective in your efforts and in the use of your resources.

Great help can be found in associations and organizations that are involved in a similar field. A quick search on the Internet will reveal that there is a support organization for any activity a person can dream up. And if there isn't one, you can always create it to connect with others who have interests similar to your own.

Help from outside your industry

Gaining a new perspective on your problem may also be helpful. Sharing a challenge with someone outside of your field may yield a fresh perspective that you may not have considered.

Several of my associates take this idea further and test some of their ideas on their children to determine if an idea is easily understood or if there is a simpler way to accomplish a task that they may have overlooked. You'll be surprised at how a child will be able to help you be more innovative, creative, or effective in finding better ways to get things done.

Whom else do you know?

As I was conducting my initial research of the world's most successful people, this question alone made more introductions possible than anything else I did. I would simply ask the person I was interviewing whom else they knew that I should talk to who could help with my research. Without fail, I would generally get two or three names and a commitment to make a personal introduction.

This magic question has introduced me to more business leaders, billionaires, celebrities, and world-class athletes than any other method. As my circle of contacts grew, so did my education, and so did my ability.

You may have heard of the idea of six degrees of separation between every person on the globe. The idea is that every person on the planet can be connected to anyone else by a distance of only six people. In other words, if you want to get to the President of the United States, you most likely know someone who knows someone who also knows someone, up until six people who knows the President of the United States. Whether this is true or not can be debated, but one thing is certain: you don't need to know every person on the globe to be successful. You only need to find a few who are willing to help you to be successful. Speaking from years of personal experience, the people you need to learn and grow from are within your reach.

Delegation

In addition to finding mentors who can help you, be on the lookout for people who can help you with the daily tasks. One afternoon I was speaking with my friend Dr. John DeMartini about success and how he maintains his. An interesting insight that John shared is worth mentioning here. Every quarter he sits down to look over what he is currently doing in his business and looks for things that he can effectively delegate. That which he delegates frees his time to focus on things only he can do or that he does best.

Delegation is not as easy as it sounds. Here are three specific considerations that you will want to be aware of as you delegate so that you will have a positive experience.

- Delegate to those you know can do the job.
- Develop effective reporting and accountability procedures.
- Delegate, but keep supervision and final say to yourself.

New business owners often suggest that they can't afford to delegate and that they must do everything personally to maintain quality. Some are even so bold as to believe they can do things just as well as others who are trained professionals. Recognize that everyone has things that they are particularly good at and things that are challenging to them. If we think we are good at everything, we obviously are not seeing the picture clearly.

In addition, if we find the right person to delegate tasks to, it is not an expense but an investment. Effective delegation should make a return of more than what it is costing. If you are currently delegating to someone who is not providing more value than you are paying for, you may want to reevaluate this relationship.

Exercise—Delegation

Make a list of the major tasks that are completed by you on a regular basis. Some of these jobs will be daily, some monthly, and some even less frequent than that.

Which of these jobs could you effectively delegate to someone else? Which of these efforts do you have to do?

As you consider delegating tasks to someone else, keep in mind that you will have to train this person to effectively handle these aspects of your business without you present. In the long run, the time invested for training will be worth it, as you will now be free to build other aspects of your business.

Write a job description and brainstorm where you might find the most effective person to help you with these tasks. Some of the areas where I have assembled people to help me include:

- marketing and promotion
- design and artwork
- social media
- public relations
- distribution of my projects
- legal and accounting
- investments
- travel and accommodation coordination

Now, of course, your business may have different needs. But I invite you to try to find a way to delegate what you can and use your unique talents to grow your success.

Do not overlook the importance of assembling a great team.

All top athletes, movies stars, and business leaders have teams that help them to be successful. In addition to the increased productivity that a well-organized team can create, there is a great blessing to have others to celebrate your success with.

When I was in China, I had the opportunity to climb one of the highest mountain peaks in all of southern China. The mountain is called Huang shan. These mountains look very much like tall skinny fingers reaching up through the clouds. The ascent is so high that you can literally see the curvature of the earth.

On one part of the mountain, ancient Buddhist monks carved out steps leading to the summit. They called it the thousand steps to heaven. And while I did not count these steps, I am confident there are more than a thousand.

We began climbing this summit from a base camp partway up the mountain at five o'clock in the morning. As we began up the mountain, one of the guides with us was an impatient man. He kept going ahead and then shouting back in Chinese, "Come on. Come on. I know the way. Come on. Come on." And he waved his arm for everyone to hurry up.

Then when we were within range, he would run ahead and yell down again, "Come on. Come on. This way. Come on." This went on through most of the morning and into the early afternoon. Finally after several hours, we stopped seeing this fellow so often.

It became apparent that he was a little frustrated with us and decided to go on ahead on his own. We continued to climb as a group at our own pace.

The day went on, and near sunset we finally reached the peak. I remember feeling incredible. I had never seen anything in nature more beautiful than this. The skyline seemed unlimited. With the clouds so far beneath us, I literally felt as though I were on the edge of the earth reaching into outer space.

My first lesson in this experience came as I turned to one of my Chinese friends and said, "Awesome. This is really awesome." He shrugged and said, "Wo bu dong." I said again, "This is awesome."

He again shrugged and repeated the same words, "Wo bu dong." "Wo bu dong" in Chinese means "I don't understand."

I tried then to describe this beautiful sight in the best Chinese I knew, "Hao, hung hao." This means, "Good, very good" in Chinese. He smiled at me and nodded. But instantly the great experience that I was having lost some of its luster. I couldn't fully share it and felt alone.

As I stood there and thought on how it would have meant more to me if I had someone to share the experience with, my Chinese friend came back to me with the others and they were all laughing. I wondered what was so funny. They then passed me some binoculars and pointed to a lower peak.

As my eyes adjusted, I saw our guide from earlier. Remember the impatient man who had continually invited us to follow him—"Come on, I know the way"? He was on a peak far below us. He had taken a wrong turn somewhere and had separated from the group. Because he had chosen to speed ahead and do things in his own way, he missed out on the opportunity to see the very top and share the experience with us.

How often are we like this in our pursuit of success? We think we know all the answers and separate ourselves from others. As a result, we miss out on the opportunity of going even higher or further than we might have as a group. We arrive at a lower location alone, where we cannot share the experience.

While I understood a little about what it was like to feel like you couldn't share an experience because of a language barrier, my feelings were probably nowhere close to what this man felt who was entirely alone. Success when it can't be shared is very empty indeed.

> Coming together is a beginning.
> Keeping together is progress.
> Working together is success.
> ——Henry Ford

Involve others—Questions to consider

- Who can I involve in my success?
- Whom might they know who can help me get to my success?
- What kind of mentors do I need?
- Where will I find them?
- How will I seek the advice?
- What can I delegate effectively?
- What can I do like my mentors do that will lead me closer to my goal?
- What am I currently doing that I could evaluate?
- Whom will I share my successes with when I arrive?

6—Reaching Success

Man is a goal seeking animal.
His life only has meaning if he is reaching
out and striving for his goals.
——Aristotle

Perseverance

*Perseverance is one of the grand differences
between greatness and what could have been.*

Recently I had a chance to spend some time with Edward James Olmos. He is known to many for his role on the television series *Battlestar Galactica* as Commander Adama. You may also recognize him from TV shows like *Miami Vice* or the movie *Blade Runner*. Edward and I chatted about the principles he felt contributed to much of his success as an actor. He said something quite fascinating to me that I had never heard before.

"Everyone says that success is a matter of doing the things that we don't like to do, even though we know we need to do them. That's true. But it's also important to do the things that we do like to do, even when we don't want to do them."

How often do we find it difficult to do the things we like to do? My observation has been more often than we admit. Not all days run smoothly, and sometimes even staying motivated to do what we really like to do can be hard.

Edward's comments reminded me of a conversation I had with an athlete not too long ago. His area of expertise was sprinting. At a certain event he did not feel like running the race. A lot of his apprehension came from fear.

There were competitors present who had beaten him in the past. He felt that a recent change in coaches left him less than prepared. He felt that the recent rain would make the track less than perfect. He tried to latch onto whatever excuse he could find. Even though running was his love, something about that day made it tough.

When we can't give our best, sometimes just showing up can make a huge difference. Perseverance is in large measure about just showing up. Sometimes the prize does not go to the most talented, but rather the one who can be counted on when the going gets tough.

Howard Putnam started out as a farm boy in Iowa. He learned how to fly airplanes from his dad. He wanted to be a pilot but found out in his teens that he was colorblind. Rather than give up his aspiration of being involved in the aviation business, he shifted gears and began to dream of becoming the president of an airline.

After high school he left Iowa for Chicago to go to college. There he got a job loading baggage onto airplanes on the midnight shift. Soon the company he worked for merged with United Airlines, and Howard remained there for the next twenty years. While at United he worked at more than thirteen different positions, each one opening more doors and elevating his stature within the company.

With a strong farm-boy work ethic, every time someone would have a job to do, Howard got the job done. This wasn't always easy, but Howard made it a rule that when a job needed to be done, he did it.

This effort did not go unnoticed, and Southwest Airlines founder Herb Kelleher recruited Howard to be his new CEO. Working hard even when the job is tough always pays off.

Is the commitment worth it?

Most people quit and give up because they lose the vision of what the final destination is. They don't recognize that perseverance is required to get to any goal. Most of the satisfying and rewarding things in life come only after commitment and hard work.

Most people who arrive at the end reward often lose their memory as to how tough it was to get there. Almost without exception, they agree that the sacrifice to get there was not really a sacrifice at all.

Exercise—Will the effort be worth the work?

Take a piece of paper and divide it down the center. On one side describe the current challenges that are required of you, and on the other side of the page describe the end goal. If this is really a goal you want, you will see that the situation you have to persevere through is temporary, and while it may be difficult, it is surmountable with effort.

Perseverance—Questions to consider

- What does perseverance mean to me?
- When will I decide to quit? Will I decide to quit?
- What will I do to stay motivated when things get tough?
- How temporary are the troubles I must go through?

Excerpts from the Success Interviews: Howard Putnam

Howard Putnam is the former CEO of the highly successful Southwest Airlines. He left Southwest to go to Braniff International, where, as CEO, he was the first executive to restructure a major airline into, through, and out of chapter 11 without any government aid.

Doug: Great to chat with you again, Howard. Let's talk about success. What is your definition of success?

Howard: I was just reading about Lucas Glover, who just won the US open golf tournament, and somebody described him as a person of purpose and not flash. That probably is not a bad description for me. I just knew when I was about twenty-one as a ticket agent at Midway in Chicago that I wanted to be the president of an airline, and I really didn't have a pathway figured out. But my philosophy, coming from the farm, was if somebody asked me to do something, I did it. And if they said, "Here's a job to do something. Who is interested?" I would raise my hand and say, "I can do that." And that's why I had thirteen different positions along the way before I was group VP of marketing. So I think perseverance was a strong factor. Integrity and honesty. I used to say—I don't say this anymore—"Open the Komono. Show me what you've got. Keep no secrets from your people, your stakeholders, your bosses, your family." And contrary to what most people say, "Don't take your work home with you." I always took my work home with me. I shared it with Krista, my wife, and Mike and Sue. And we talked about it at home and kept them involved as well. I think that is important in the longevity of marriage. We're coming up on fifty-two years.

Doug: Congratulations! That's great.

Howard: Not too many of those around. So perseverance, integrity, and I had a passion. I wanted to be a president of an airline. And I enjoyed people. I never stepped on anybody to get to the next level. If I could do the job, I did. Sometime ago somebody said, "How did you know that you could compete against other people?" My answer was that I figured out that 50 percent of the people had no clue what they wanted to do in life. So therefore, I only had to compete against 50 percent. And out of the 50 percent, I figured I could do better than half of them could. So therefore I only had to compete against 25 percent of the working population. And that seemed like a pretty easy task.

Doug: In your journey to success, what has been your number one obstacle, and how did you overcome it?

Howard: Number one obstacle was probably being impetuous and too impatient at times. And not doing as thorough due diligence as I should have. And probably that was an error before I left Southwest and went to Braniff. I saw an opportunity and got excited about the opportunity. I probably should have drilled down a little deeper before I made the decision.

Doug: Now, Howard, you have been in charge of managing a significant number of people at times. How have you been able to inspire them to reach for greater things in their areas of responsibility?

Howard: One thing I learned, and it took me a while to learn this: not everyone wants to be inspired to go on to a higher job or more responsibility. Some people are very content staying at the level that they are. So you have got to manage them differently than those that have the ambition that I had to move ahead. Example, when I was thirty-five years old, I was the vice president of passenger marketing for United Airlines, based in Chicago. I had a vice president of advertising who reported to me, and he was probably in his midfifties. So he had me by twenty years. He was a horrible manager. Great at advertising. Creative, etcetera. He was the one who saw the wisdom in the greatest airline slogan ever, "Fly the friendly skies of United," and got the ad agency to present it to senior management and get it through. But what I was doing incorrectly was trying to make him a good manager of his people and be an administrator and all that, and I was killing his creativity. So I finally saw the error of my ways. And I brought him in the office, and I said, "Fred, here's what we are going to do. We are going to hire an office manager to take all this stuff off of your plate. And you focus on creativity and advertising." And he hugged me and cried. It startled me. I was putting so much pressure on the guy. So I learned there, you cannot manage everyone the same.

Try to look at an individual, see inside of them and what their own goals and aspirations are, and then guide them along that path. Be open with them. People often talk about performance evaluations; you must have goals and so forth. And I agree with that. But you've really got to keep it simple for people, and often we give too many goals and there is no way they can achieve all of them and they get frustrated and give up. So when I was at Southwest, I put in a very simple system for all of the vice presidents, director levels, and manager levels. One-third of their annual evaluation was based on how the total company did, revenue and bottom line. And of course, they would say immediately, "Wait a minute, I am in charge of customer service; that doesn't have anything to do with maintenance and pilots." And I would say, "I don't care. We all work for Southwest Airlines. So one-third of your evaluation is how well you work with the team to make it happen for the company." The second third, you and I will agree on only three measurable goals for the year, for the fiscal year. They have got to be able to be revenue-measured or cost-measured or productivity-measured. They can't be subjective. And the final third is subjective. It's how you and I get along together. How I see you in the community. How I see you leading your people, which is totally subjective. Well, the first year that was pretty difficult to implement. Some people were not believers. But when they saw a young guy, Tom Bolz, the VP of marketing, get the biggest bonus, 'cause he really understood what I was talking about, the second year it was a breeze in managing that group of people. Manage people within their value systems.

Doug: From a management perspective then, how do you manage people that are difficult?

Howard: Again, by way of example. We had a young man in San Francisco, and I was the VP out there in charge of customer service. This young man was truly a pain in the ass. Every meeting we had, he was the first one with his hand up; he was always complaining about something. We have too many lost bags, we have too many complaints from customers, we have this, we have that—nothing was ever right. I sat down with his boss, and I said, "This guy's got a lot of talent. We are missing something in this. We have got to find another niche for him; we've got him misplaced. He's ticking everybody off, including you and me." And one of us came up with the idea; I don't remember who. "Let's put him in charge of lost bags and complaints. He thinks they're such big issues. Let him figure it out." So we did. And the guy was outstanding. In fact, I think he won employee of the year the following year. So we were able to match him with a skill set; he was a hard person to get along with, but we were able to match his skill sets and his attitude with something he could really do well with.

So I haven't had too many people over the years that were just complete jerks; if they were, we just fired them. Now there is one different dimension there. We always said at Southwest we hired attitudes and we teach them skills. Hire attitudes and teach them skills. Hire attitudes that fit your culture. If you do that and you get the folks that are all the right ones on the same team, they will apply peer pressure to those that are not performing. And seldom at Southwest Airlines did we ever have to terminate anybody. Peer pressure was so great. And we had profit sharing, so people would just go to somebody who was dogging it and say, "Come on, you're screwing us all. So either get with the program or get out." And it worked. They still do it today.

Doug: From a leader's point of view, what advice would you have in terms of delegation?

Howard: The first thing is that the vision of the company and organization has to be simple and very clear. We wrote a vision statement at Southwest Airlines that is only forty letters long. It was kind of strategic; it was kind of tactical. But it just simply said, "We are not an airline; we are mass transportation." Vision has got to be clear and succinct. That's the first thing. Second, you have got to understand what business you are in. Transportation. We were a cattle car. Third piece is now that you understand what business you are in, how do you create a culture to support the value proposition? How do you get the customers to say, "I didn't get any first class, I didn't get any seat assignment, I didn't get any meals. But the flight was on time, the people were friendly," and that kept them coming back all the time. And that supported the value of proposition. If those three are clear, then it's pretty easy to sit down with your managers and define what it is you are going to delegate to them.

Capital expenditures was a big thing with the airline. At the beginning of the year, we would lay out how many tractors, how many tugs, how many carts we thought we would have to buy, city by city. And it was a pretty detailed analysis, and I never said to the managers, "You can go ahead and buy that next June." I always said, "You need to come back one more time because conditions may have changed between now and June. Yes, it is in the plan, but it is not your money to spend. It is the company's and the shareholders' money, and we'll make the decision together." So that's one thing that we made very clear. I am not delegating that to you. The other ones that were also very clear were that we developed clear standards of: How many passengers one employee could board in a day? How many bags can one employee load in a day? And we came up with performance standards which then made it very easy to say to a manager, "You've got twelve flights a day in this schedule change. We know pretty much that your load factor will be 72 percent. That tells you how many passengers. Break it down by flight, by shift, and you can figure out how much manpower you need." And they were on their own.

So the vision needs to be clear, figure out what business you're in, what is the value proposition that the culture is going to support, and then you can go ahead and make your decisions on delegation pretty easily from there.

Doug: So with all the things you have been able to accomplish, what have you done to stay continually successful?

Howard: I have had some failures along the way that helped me become better the next time. I have started three little companies over the last twenty years. One of them didn't make it, and one of them was just average. So I will go back and analyze what my mistakes were. One company was involved in seat repair for airlines. And it did great until 9-11 came. Then the airline industry just stopped refurbishing seats and interiors. So we all had to, as entrepreneurs—there were seven of us that owned the company—had to kick in a lot more money. I had not planned on doing that. That did not go over well at the dinner table. But we made a commitment to each other that we were going to make this thing succeed. Well, we went on for another three or four years after pouring more money in it. Finally we all said, "We've got to sell this thing and give up the ghost. It was a good idea. But it ain't working." And that's probably one of the hardest decisions for anybody to make is, the old Kenny Rogers' song, "you got to know when to hold 'em and you got to know when to fold 'em." And most of us, including me in that situation, waited too long to fold 'em. And it cost me a hell of a lot of money. But out of that, I learned that next time I start something or invest in something, my criteria are going to be a little clearer. And I will not be as impatient, and I will not be as impetuous. And I will think it through further and deeper.

Doug: So as an entrepreneur, what would you suggest would be the most important thing an entrepreneur should know or understand before heading into business?

Howard: What the business schools will tell you is that you must have a sound business plan. And I have seen a lot of sound business plans that were baloney. They have all the right ingredients, but your intuition just tells you that it isn't going to work. And I have had three or four of those that I have been advisers to folks and mentoring in the dot com era, and I finally decided that these things have such short product cycles that I am just not going to waste my time on these. I don't understand them well enough to be giving people good advice. So I say to those guys, "Young people, you may understand your idea, but I don't understand it well enough that I am willing to be on your board of directors, and I don't understand it well enough that I am willing to put in my own money. And I don't understand it enough that I am going to go and help you raise money. So if you believe in it, you're going to have to go and do it by yourself. Because somebody like me is from a different generation; I can't see it with you." And they kind of look at you teary-eyed, like … "but this is my idea." And it may be. But one out of twenty of those actually work. So my advice is that if you have an idea for business and you've been around a little and people say I just can't get with it, maybe you ought to just give up the ghost and go on and do something else. Again, know when to fold 'em.

Doug: That's really important. Ownership of an idea doesn't necessarily guarantee success of an idea. People often hold more to the idea than to take the time to see why it won't work or reshape it into something that will work.

Howard: Often people are ahead of their time with an idea. And maybe you just put it in the closet for a while and think about it. You look at people like Henry Ford, who went bankrupt before he invented the Model T. I don't know how many times Walt Disney failed at business. But the other side of the equation is that maybe your idea is not the one that's going to make it, but don't stop thinking about ideas. Keep looking; you may find the magic one sometime down the road.

New Heights

Our purpose is progress.
Our progress reflects our purpose.

Now that you have reached the summit of the achievement, you may wonder what to do next. It feels great to be here, but what next? You can only stand in the spotlight of your last victory for so long. We all know people who like to talk about the good ol' days when they were the all-star quarterback or the prom queen or the guy who made ten big sales last week. Life is not about what happened last year or last week. It's about what is happening now.

Yesterday's successes are like stale moldy bread. At one time they were great. But few people are excited to hear about it today. Unless you are feeding your mind with new stimulus, you will feel the exciting feelings of past accomplishments slip away.

There was a study done on the needs of the human mind. The needs that rated most highly were challenge and stimulation. Humans thrive on finding solutions to challenging situations. It is only in seeking these new and more fulfilling outcomes that we can continue to have enriching variety in our lives.

New Heights—Questions to consider

- What more can I do with this experience?
- What can I do next?
- How can I apply what I have just learned to create even greater victories?
- What new problems are there that I can solve with this success?
- How can I improve on this successful situation?

Excerpts from the Success Interviews: Trent Carlini

Trent Carlini is the world's number one Elvis Presley tribute artist. Trent performs for thousands of people each year in Las Vegas. Trent has appeared on *Entertainment Tonight, NBC Nightline, Late Night with David Letterman, The Oprah Winfrey Show, ABC Primetime,* and other TV shows.

Most recently Trent won the impersonator reality show on ABC's *The Next Best Thing.*

Doug: What does success mean to you? What is the definition of success?

Trent: Well, for me the definition of success is really having had the opportunity to engage in what I have wanted. Ever since I was young, I had this focus point to want to be just like what Elvis Presley had been in the music industry. And I modeled myself to the point where I was actually able to take on the performance of the Elvis show.

Doug: What would you say have been contributing factors to your success?

Trent: Well, I think just on a step-by-step level, the first thing was that I went to music school, and I tried to learn the three major points that I needed to know to take on this venture. One was learning how to play the guitar. Second, learn how to sing. And lastly, learn how to be a performer on stage. Putting those three elements together, I was able to perform in certain places, which gave me the ability to keep moving forward. And I think the key performance was when I came to Las Vegas to perform the tribute show. I think that was my first really big opportunity. I think a factor of success is passion, the passion that a person has to do something. Nothing will stop me. I always felt inside that I had the ability to accomplish my goals. And I had the passion. I wouldn't let anyone detour me from where I wanted to go and what I wanted to be.

There were a lot of negative people along the way. They would say, "You can't do this. There are so many people that do this already." But I always felt that, "No, I am going to do this, and it's going to be special." I was very focused on reaching my goal. My original goal that I set way, way back when I started was that I wanted to work with everyone who had worked with Elvis and I wanted to perform where he had performed. And once I reached that goal, I set another goal a lot higher. Because the first one I was able to achieve in a short period. My goal became to produce events around the world and to perform in very large venues. And not only that, but set up an organization where I could help other E.T.A. (Elvis tribute artists) in their performing and share the knowledge I spent the last twenty years accumulating.

Doug: What has been the most challenging obstacle for you, and how did you overcome it?

Trent Well, some of the biggest obstacles I had were not in the music field, but were personal situations. Sometimes I found myself surrounded with people that were not always conducive to my vision or my career and what I was doing. And they didn't always believe in what I was doing. They were just along for the ride. And I've had a few setbacks because of that, by allowing people of negative influence to have their say. But what pulled me out of it was to focus again on the music part of it and my vision and the performing. I have to say, looking back in my life, everything that has ever happened to me that has been good has come out of working hard at what I do. When you know exactly what you want, you can overcome any obstacle. You will have setbacks and you will have bumps, you will come out a little bruised here and there, but overall when you know what you want, it's like having a life vest. The life vest of success around you will keep you afloat until you reach the island.

Doug: What advice would you give to someone wanting to be successful, whether in business or in their personal life?

Trent: From my experiences again, it's important to keep the enthusiasm. Once you have reached a certain level of success, don't stop. Don't stop to watch your success. Enjoy that ride. Keep going. Never stop. Keep going and going and going. Because once you stop, it is harder to start again. Procrastination kicks in. You will always have people telling you how much they enjoy the show, and it's beautiful to hear that, but there are some people that stop and focus on hearing that over and over and over. Seeking praise keeps you from focusing on the end goal. As we speak, I have producers working on new segments for the show, musical directors looking for new songs to sing, people working on new costumes to wear. New concepts. We keep bending the show in new directions so there is always freshness. So my advice is to never stop. No matter what level of success you are at. You can reach success beyond comprehension. But don't stop. If you take just one action a day, that's 365 actions a year. But they are not just by themselves. They compound. They multiply. And everything changes to a higher level.

Making It Personal

If you haven't put your personal unique stamp on your success, you are not finished yet.

You may have heard it said that everyone has a book within him or her to write. At first I didn't believe it. I thought that even I really didn't have anything very interesting to say. But the more I looked at my own experience and the experiences of others, the more I have come to realize how genuinely unique and interesting each person is.

In the same way, no one has the exact same goal and desires as you do. There is no one with exactly the same gifts and abilities as you have. Everyone has a unique story.

When I first started as a speaker, I was teaching a seminar, and one of the participants asked me a question I was not prepared for. The question was: "After your studies of the world's four hundred top achievers and most successful people, what was the most important ingredient that they *had* that made them succeed?"

I tried to answer at first by describing something that they *did*. But the man who asked the question said that's not what he meant. He said he understood what they *did*, but wanted to know what they *had*. I listened more carefully. This was an interesting question.

I stood there and thought for a moment about their backgrounds, circumstances, financial situations, relationships, and education. There was only one common thing that they all had. They were all unique. It was their uniqueness that had helped them develop success in their particular field. They understood how to tap into their gifts, talents, and unique passions, and that is what made them successful.

It was also not a matter of them being different and trying different things. It was a matter of them knowing how to use those unique differences for maximum gain. They might do what others do, but they would then take it a step further by utilizing their gifts and abilities to do the things that others perhaps could not do. I call that stepping into your brilliance zone. Your greatest success will also come as you build in your area of uniqueness.

Personal Attachment

By making their goal highly personal, these top achievers also found a special attachment that can never appear when the goal is borrowed or comes at the command of someone else. A sense of ownership and internal connection will always bring additional strengths to the surface that would otherwise go unnoticed. This same journey is available to you.

Making it personal—Questions to consider

- What unique contribution can I make?
- After following the regular course, what can I add to make it mine?
- What makes this goal unique to me?
- What will I do differently from others who have sought this goal?

Excerpts from the Success Interviews: Michael Israel

The next step in the evolution of art, entertainment, and humanitarianism, —Michael Israel blends the excitement of art and combines it with the thrill of a rock concert. Michael has created art for a variety of events, including the inauguration events for President Barak Obama, the Olympic Games, celebrity events, and significant charitable fund-raising events. To see Michael create one of his magical masterpieces is an experience that cannot be put into words.

From canvasses spinning, brushes and paint zipping every which way, splatters and sprinkles of paint leaping rhythmically in the air, to intense music that gets the whole place pumping, Michael Israel is incredible.

To see what I am talking about, go to www.MichaelIsrael.com.

Doug: How I'd like to begin, if we could, Michael, is to have you give a little bit of a background on yourself, with some of the highlights and please tell us about your martial arts background.

Michael: The martial arts training is really paramount to everything else that I do. I was very fortunate to meet a great instructor when I was about twelve. I'd actually started when I was about eight, but the man I call my sensei, he was pretty much a fanatic. He was also dying of leukemia, so he had a pretty interesting thrust and viewpoint on life. And no matter what level you were at or how good you were, you were still a punk, and there was still room for improvement. So we trained extremely hard at the school, and interestingly enough, if you went to an event and there were two thousand people there, you could literally pick out each one of his students without ever having met them before. They would be the ones standing at attention or sitting formally, perfectly still, very respectful, very traditional. They were also the ones who came home with all the trophies at the end of the day. Our guys used to have to fight it out for first, second, and third place. So he was a tremendous influence.

Doug: So how did that lead into becoming involved with art?

Michael: Well, I had always been interested in art. I think part of the play was that I was really interested in dragons and I didn't like the way anyone else was painting them so I used to paint them all the time. And that kind of led into some other things. But the martial arts training makes you very focused. And it makes you very fast in a lot of ways and also reactive. One of the things in martial arts training is to react like a pool of water, so whatever action is coming towards you, react like a mirror without even thinking about it. It sort of just happens. So that's how a lot of the artwork is with a certain level of training; a lot of what I do just happens. And because there is a skill level behind it, I can put an eighth of an inch dot of paint on a spinning canvas exactly where I want it to land.

Doug: So how much preparation do you put into each piece of artwork before you get on stage and create it in front of an audience?

Michael: About thirty-five years.

Doug: How profound and true.

Michael: Actually about sixteen hours a day on the average. I used to paint till I had blisters on my fingers. I used to literally keep a bucket of ice water and soak my hand in it. Until I found that it was bad for me I used to eat aspirins and Tylenols by the handful.

Doug: That's certainly not something most people think about when they see you perform. You make it look so easy and effortless and gracious. But there definitely is a lot of work and effort that has gone in. I really like your first answer of thirty-five years, because I really don't think a lot of people consider how much of your life you've dedicated to developing this gift.

Michael: The real honesty behind it is I have probably put in more time painting than most artists will do in several lifetimes. I was the guy who was up at four in the morning painting until I fell down basically. Same way I did my karate training. We went until we passed out. And he'd come over and tell you he'd kick you if you didn't get back up. You train. You train. Everything you have within you is given.

Doug: How did you get started in the concert performance of art? How did you get started down that road instead of just becoming a painter?

Michael: Well, I used to paint at festivals as a kid, and what would happen is I would not necessarily have a bunch of work that people would pick and say, "I want that one." I would have blank canvases and people would hand me pictures of what they wanted. You know, this is my grandfather from World War II, this is our cat, this is our boat, whatever it happened to be. Very long days, so I would have the music cranking real loud to keep me going. I'd line up three or four artworks at a time. And go at it like someone possessed to the rhythm of the music. Half the time I would finish paintings and not even realize I had done them. In the process I would have crowds as far back as I could see watching me paint. I used to think if I could have a dollar from everybody watching, I could give the artwork away. It kind of developed.

Doug: What has been the most exciting piece of artwork you have created?

Michael: The next one. There have been a lot of amazing times, though. Whether it's performing for homecoming wounded soldiers that have given their body parts and their lives or to help out for the Special Olympics. Any number of things. The works where more comes out of the artwork than what goes into it are my favorite, and what I mean by that is, the works that affect lives in a better way. Whether it's educational, fund-raising, or just helping heal wounds, so to speak. Those are the magical pieces. Those are the masterpieces.

Doug: So what has been the most challenging piece you have created so far?

Michael: Well, the recent Warren Buffet piece was challenging. But only because the paint was supposed to have been kept warm indoors until just before the performance. It was thirty degrees out. So here I am on stage about to perform the painting of the world's richest man, and it's announced that I am going to do this in eight minutes before a bleacher full of the press from around the world. And I go to stick my brushes in the paint and pull out two pudding pops. I pretty much thought that was the end of my career, and I still think it must have been divine intervention that actually helped the painting come out as good as it did. I still don't know how I did it.

Doug: Well, that painting looked great. I can imagine that's something that taught you from now on that the paint must be more carefully supervised beforehand.

Michael: I actually knew about that in advance. I learned that on my trip to the Winter Olympics. Painting on the medals stage. They asked me on the plane ride over there, "By the way, does your paint freeze?" and I said, "Why? Are we outside?" I learned then that you do need to keep the paint warm. And it was supposed to happen that way at the Warren Buffet event. But in this super bowl of business meetings, things were pretty hectic during the setup and all, and I guess people got sidetracked. I mean, I've got a great stage crew, but a lot was going on.

Doug: What do you do to stay continually at the top of your game?

Michael: I always try to be better than I am. I train three to six days a week physically. In fact, we are doing a photo shoot this weekend to kind of show people how hard the physical training is that I do. Because I don't think there is an artist on the planet that does what I do. I mean, there are athletes that train as hard. I'm in tears through most of my workouts.

Doug: So what would be the number one reason you think you are successful?

Michael: I give more than I take.

Doug: So what is your definition of success?

Michael: Significance. Moving forward in a significant manner. Because repeating the same success of something you have already done loses its significance when you keep doing it over and over. Like the same meal. Or like the same race. Every time you raise the bar and you do something of some significance a little bit better, you are happy. I mean, that's easy to say, it's human nature. Success and happiness basically come from the same thing. It's not how much you make, it's how you do it. The significance of what you're doing. Because you can find billionaires that aren't really happy with the next thing they've done, and you can probably find a homeless person that is happy with a thing that they have done.

Doug: So in getting to your success, what has been your biggest challenge or obstacle, and how did you overcome it?

Michael: The biggest challenge has been communicating my vision to people who can't see it. Any great visionary sees things that other people don't see. This person has this vision, and it's not great until others see that vision.

Doug: How did you get other people to see your vision?

Michael: It's a work in progress.

Doug: What advice would you give to others wanting to get to their success?

Michael: I would say, "Do something that makes you feel like every day is Christmas Eve." Meaning you can't wait to get up in the morning to work on what you're going to work on. It doesn't matter how much you make. If you follow that, you'll be happy. You'll always go to bed at night with a passion for the next day. If you are watching the clock or concerned about other things and you have no passion, you are going to be miserable. Achievement in and of itself is not success.

Give More Than You Take

When we give, we also make more room to receive.

One of the most impressive common denominators of the most successful people is their ability to give more than they take. Motivational guru Zig Ziglar is well-known for his philosophy, "The best way to get what you want is to help someone else to get what they want first."

While these thoughts appear near the end of this book, they could have quite as easily been placed at the beginning of the book. Success is a matter of recognizing and servicing the needs of others. If you don't see great success in your life, you might want to look at how well you are servicing the needs of others.

Self-serving or selfish motives very rarely create a success that reaches beyond yourself. When we give, we get. Have you ever noticed that when our hand is closed tightly to hold onto something, our closed hand also keeps us from receiving anything new?

> You give but little when you give of your possessions.
> It is when you give of yourself that you truly give.
> —Kahlil Gibran

Give more than you take—Questions to consider

- What am I doing to help other people in their situations?
- How am I becoming a contributor?
- What is my success leaving as a fingerprint that I was there?
- What can I contribute to others around me today?
- What area of service can be improved in my life?

7—Bonus Guerrilla Ideas

Some extra suggestions to speed the process of getting to your goals!

Continual Learning Plan

When we learn more, we increase our capacity to accomplish more.

Shortly after the last day of high school, I was riding my bike in a forested area near my home at dusk. As I came down a hill, I recognized a group of teenagers I knew from my school. They were sitting around a big blazing bonfire.

As I got closer, I saw piles of notebooks and school supplies sitting on a nearby picnic table. As I stopped my bike in curiosity, I asked, "What's the occasion?"

"School's out. And this is the party," one of my friends said as he lobbed another notebook onto the fire. As I observed more carefully, I noticed that not everyone had brought books to burn. I asked one of the fellows where his books were. His reply: "I am going to need mine; I have to go back for college in the fall."

Many people feel that learning is only necessary when we are forced to learn, or when there is a specific reason for the learning. If there is no reason, learning has no point. Top achievers recognize the opposite is true. As we are continually learning, the opportunities to apply that knowledge will appear. These opportunities are the situations that lead to progress and promotion.

Where you were will not get you to where you're going.

Exercise—Find something to learn.

I invite you to accept the challenge to become a continual learner. Seek experiences and opportunities that will teach you and prepare you to become better. Find something that you would like to explore and begin to learn about it. It doesn't need to be related to your business or career. Let it be something you enjoy and something that stimulates and challenges your brain.

By doing so, you will find greater ideas and new insights about the things you are currently working on.

> The purpose of learning is growth, and our minds,
> unlike our bodies, can continue growing as long as we live.
> ——Mortimer Adler

Continual learning plan—Questions to consider

- What skills would have helped my achievement process?
- What else would I like to learn?
- Where will I go for continual learning?
- What do I need to learn so that I can be considered for promotion?
- What do those already in positions I want understand?
- What increased education can I attain?

Goal Journal

If you don't record the exciting events of your life, who will?

I keep two journals.

I keep a journal every day. It helps me to remember experiences and see progress I have made. Oftentimes when things go wrong in my life or I experience challenges, my journal is a great source of strength. I use it to remind myself of past successes and to remember that even my past success came with some struggle.

The second journal I keep is a goal journal. Keeping a goal journal is somewhat different than a daily journal. While a daily journal records experiences that have happened, a goal journal records plans and inspiration about things that will happen.

In my goal journal, I include photos of things I want to do, telephone numbers of people I need to contact who can help me, and ideas of things that I can do to make my accomplishment of my goals easier.

I often carry this journal around with me during the day. As I encounter something that might help me get to my goals, I write it down. I have found that keeping the size of this journal to something that can fit in my pocket helps, because having it with me all the time has been a key to staying on track with important goals.

Review regularly.

Now it is one thing to write in a journal. It is another thing to take some time and read in it. Review what you have written and follow up on the information you have recorded. Sort it out into information you can use now and later. I admit that most of what I record, I will never use. But because I record it, I never lose it. It is always there for future consideration. And much like the exercise of brainstorming, I can sift through and find the nuggets that are most valuable. The more ideas I record, the more ideas I have.

A tool to keep you focused

Having a journal like this with you all the time can also help to keep you focused. I would be considered by many people to be afflicted with ADD (attention deficit disorder). Personally I think it is a blessing overall, but at times there is a bit of a challenge.

Each new and interesting idea that comes my way generally calls out for my attention. My mind and heart want to do everything and help everyone. And that is just not possible.

I have tried to train my mind to go directly for my journal and write down the thoughts that I have. Instead of making a commitment to get involved in every new thing, I simply commit to write it down. I can then step away, and when I am not in the heat of the excitement, I can revisit my notes. In a calm setting, I can determine which of the projects I would like to dedicate some of my time to. In many cases, as I am reading, I am reminded of my number one mission, and my focus returns back to where I need it to be.

Your journal will be interesting.

Lastly, I encourage everyone to keep a journal because it is a record of your life. It shares who you are, what you felt, thought, and did. One day, especially after you are gone, others will follow after you who will find it interesting to know about your failures and successes. The methods you used to create success could be very valuable to your grandchildren, great-grandchildren, and so on.

In our family we have records from many of my ancestors, and many of the experiences that they had have been an inspiration to me. You could give the same gift to those who will follow you.

> In Hollywood now when people die they don't say,
> "Did he leave a will?" but "Did he leave a diary?"
> —Liza Minnelli

Goal journal—Questions to consider

- Do I have a goal journal?
- Am I using it?
- Do I carry it with me throughout the day?
- What will I record?
- When will I review the material I've written in my journal?

Kindness and Gratitude

The most incredible changes in the world begin in the hearts of regular men.

Your first thought might have been, "What's this section doing in a book about getting to your goals?" What do kindness and gratitude have to do with creating success? A lot actually.

Let's talk first about kindness. Common sense demonstrates that this single principle alone will increase productivity in the workplace, generate more leads for your business, make for stronger marriages and better relationships with your children, and gives more inner peace than meditating. And it's so simple.

So simple that it is easy to forget how important it is and to think that it really doesn't matter. It matters far more than any recognition we have given it up until this point. I hope that will change for you today.

When we reach out to others in kindness, they are willing to help us get to our goals and become interested in seeing us succeed. It's as simple as that. While it has been said that nice guys finish last, it's important to notice that they actually get to finish. Difficult and stubborn people often get somewhere in life, but they often only get to do it once or twice. As soon as people catch on that they are difficult to deal with, they are denied further opportunities. Their dreams remain unfinished.

It is nice to be important, but it is more important to be nice. Treat everyone with politeness and kindness, even those who are rude to you—not because they are nice, but because you are. You can choose your response, and it will make all the difference for you.

Consider when you have had a blowup or a negative experience with someone. How easy has it been to get back to work and keep your focus on the things you need to do? It never is. And the more you let those feelings brew, the less productive you will be. We work at our best capacity when we are in positive circumstances.

Mark Twain said, "Kindness is the language which the deaf can hear and the blind can see." I have literally seen those who were deaf hear my ideas and those who were blind see my vision literally open up as I have approached them with a sincere heart and kind expressions. You truly do get more with sugar than vinegar, as the saying goes.

Be likable.

In the same direction as being nice is the importance of being likable. Recently I was sitting with my dad talking about some of the principles in this book as I prepared for press. He shared a story that I knew needed to be included:

There was a man whom he worked with who was very intelligent. He had performed his job well, he knew much about his industry, and he followed company procedure in every detail. He was in almost all respects a model worker. But this man never got a promotion or advancement. It wasn't that he didn't apply. He did. In fact, he applied for every promotion that came along. So why didn't he get promotions?

The reason my dad told me was that he wasn't likable. The bosses didn't want him around, and neither did any of the other workers. A dark cloud followed this fellow everywhere he went. Although he got his job done, he was a complainer, he found fault, and he was always argumentative. Part of success is learning how to be liked. Be the kind of person whom people want to be around, and you will find you get invited to participate in greater opportunities to be involved.

Exercise—Kindness

The exercise for kindness is simple. Just do it. Be kind and try to be less selfish in everything you do. Look for ways to be even kinder and gentler with people. You may not start out perfect, but the more you can develop this attribute, the more you will recognize the benefits of it.

Exercise—Speak kind words.

Sometimes it is very easy to speak your mind about things and people you do not agree with. I have done it, often without thinking of the consequences. It has led to regret and challenge. When you criticize or try to hold another person down through your thoughts, words, and actions, you will also hold a part of yourself back in the process. Set a goal to speak only kind words about others, even if you feel they don't deserve them.

Gratitude

Gratitude is an important point of view. When we look at things with gratitude, we enable ourselves to solve problems in a better way. We also begin to attract better things in our own lives. When we are filled with gratitude, selfishness flees and we begin to see things in a different light.

One of the big challenges with many people is that they are so focused on what they can acquire next that they don't enjoy or utilize what they currently have. On the flip side of that, many people focus so much on what they don't have that what they do have loses all value.

If we can learn to recognize and appreciate what we currently have, we can use it to build more. Our gratitude will then have the power to affect our entire life in a positive way. (For more on the power of gratitude, be sure to check out my film *The Gratitude Experiment*, www. TheGratitudeExperiment.com.)

> As we express our gratitude, we must never forget that the highest appreciation is not to utter words, but to live by them.
> —John F. Kennedy

Exercise—Gratitude

Sometimes when things seem to be going horribly wrong, it is really easy to say, "There is absolutely nothing to be grateful for." This is never true. As long as you are breathing, you can find something to be grateful for.

My friend Laurie Davis shares this exercise. Try for a moment to sit still, close your eyes, and imagine that you just stepped outside of your house or office, and everything around you has disappeared. Even the clothes on your back are gone, and you are sitting in a field with absolutely nothing— naked. (And yes, you are alone so you don't have to worry about being embarrassed.) Even begin by holding your breath.

As you sit there alone, start to list the things that you are grateful for, and as you mention them, they reappear in your life. (I would encourage you to start with your breath—get that back right away. It's somewhat important.) Start working on the other things. It's my suspicion that it won't take you very long to find that you have many things to be grateful for. When you find things to be grateful for, your perspective will change and gratitude will grow in your life.

> Let us rise up and be thankful, for if we didn't learn a lot today,
> at least we learned a little,
> and if we didn't learn a little, at least we didn't get sick,
> and if we got sick, at least we didn't die;
> so, let us all be thankful.
> —Buddha

Kindness and gratitude—Questions to consider

- Whom can I be kind to right now?
- How can I stop being critical of others?
- How can I apply kindness to the difficult situations I am currently facing?
- What can I be grateful for right now?
- How can I utilize the things I currently have in my life to create more?

There Are No Small Moments

The key to happiness is having dreams.
The key to success is making your dreams come true.
—James Allen

The consequences of your life can be shaped by what you choose to do and what you choose to ignore. These decisions will generally be the moments that no one else can see, but they will have a profound effect on your entire life.

The lesson of the Great Wall

One of my dreams since I was a little boy had been to visit the Great Wall of China. When I was in China, I made a point of visiting the wall. It was an incredible experience to stand on this magnificent structure.

It goes on and on for miles and miles. It has been said that it is the only man-made structure that is visible from outer space.

As I stood on the Great Wall, I had a startling revelation. As I looked from side to side to see how far this magnificent structure stretched, I stopped and looked at my feet. Underneath my feet were the bricks the wall is made from. They are small bricks. Some of the bricks are only about three inches by eight inches long. Everywhere I walked along the wall, these bricks were under my feet.

As I walked along the wall, I looked up again. It was then that a light bulb went on in my mind; the entire Great Wall is made up of these same small bricks. As I stood in awe of this realization, I thought on how much this is similar to our lives. The great things in our lives are the right combination of the little bricks, or smaller moments. By placing these smaller bricks in the right positions in our lives, we can create magnificent structures.

My challenge to you in these final moments of this book is to make something wonderful of yourself. Look for the small moments. Take advantage of these small moments. As you build your successes and pursue your accomplishments, always remember that there are no small moments. Everything counts.

How we spend our days is how we will spend our lives.

There are no small moments—Questions to consider

- What small moments am I letting pass me by?
- What opportunities am I neglecting?
- What small moments could I seize today?
- What things am I considering small that are really not?

Biographies

About Douglas Vermeeren

Considered by many to be the modern-day Napoleon Hill, Douglas Vermeeren conducted extensive research into more than four hundred of the world's top achievers.

Doug is a recognized expert on achievement and recently returned from a year in China, where he was the first North American to ever be invited to speak to the Chinese Political Party in communist China on motivation and achievement. While there, the Wu Zhai University awarded him the distinction of visiting professor.

Doug is also the producer behind the personal development films *The Opus* and *The Gratitude Experiment*. You can find out more at www. TheOpusMovie.com and www.TheGratitudeExperiment.com.

Doug's primary coaching and mentoring program is focused on creating greater success in the field of sales and business growth.

www.TheSalesTrainer.com

Want to Have Douglas Vermeeren
Speak at Your Next Event?

To have Doug speak at your next event, contact:
Rachel@DouglasVermeeren.com.

Doug Vermeeren has the ability to motivate and inspire people to achieve their biggest *dreams*.

—**William Farley, CEO, Fruit of the Loom**

Doug Vermeeren knows what he's talking about. He's dynamic and wise and definitely worth listening to.

—**Marci Shimoff, featured teacher in The Secret and number one** New York Times **best-selling author**

Douglas Vermeeren's coaching program The Monthly Millionaire Mentor is second to none! If you want results, you've come to the right place!

—**M. Benoit, Phoenix, AZ**

Doug Vermeeren inspires others to reach their greatest potential.

—**Synchronicity Magazine**

There are *measurable things* that I actually do differently every day because of one of his talks. And I have also been able to use his tools to get actual real-world results—not just motivation. My vote also goes for Vermeeren as the #1 personal development teacher in the business today.

—**GK, reported on the Law of Attraction Blog**

You must hear this man speak!

—**Marilyn Rose, Spirit Whispers Consulting**

He has made *an extremely incredible difference* in our family and especially with my son. I won't get into details, but I will say in no uncertain terms that he has had an effect on my son that has literally changed his life (maybe even to the point of saving it.) My vote is 100 percent for Vermeeren as the strongest personal development teacher (and especially for our family) of all time.

—**Barry H., Chandler, AZ**

Well put together, and if you want a new outlook, he's the man.

—**Kelli W., Cold Lake, AB**

Jay Conrad Levinson is the author of the best-selling marketing series in history, *Guerrilla Marketing*, plus fifty-eight other business books. His books have sold more than 20 million copies worldwide. His guerrilla concepts have influenced marketing so much that his books appear in sixty-two languages and are required reading in MBA programs worldwide.

He was born in Detroit, raised in Chicago, and graduated from the University of Colorado. His studies in psychology led him to advertising agencies, including a directorship at Leo Burnett in London, where he served as creative director. Returning to the United States, he joined J. Walter Thompson as senior VP. Jay created and taught guerrilla marketing for ten years at the extension division of the University of California in Berkeley.

A winner of first prizes in all the media, he has been part of the creative teams that made household names of the Marlboro Man, the Pillsbury Doughboy, Allstate's good hands, United's friendly skies, the Sears Diehard battery, Morris the Cat, Tony the Tiger, and the Jolly Green Giant.

Today, *Guerrilla Marketing* is most powerful brand in the history of marketing. It is listed among the one hundred best business books ever written. Its popular website at www.gmarketing.com powers The Guerrilla Marketing Association, a support system for small business.

After living in the San Francisco Bay Area for thirty-five years, Jay and Jeannie Levinson sold their home, bought an RV, towed a Jeep, and ended up, six years later, at their lakefront home outside Orlando, Florida, close to their twenty-six grandchildren, their own personal Disney World. There is no better person anywhere able to tell you what you ought to know about guerrilla marketing than the father of guerrilla marketing, Jay Conrad Levinson.